ISBN 978-0-282-96382-8
PIBN 10874612

1911
K28

UNIVERSITY OF ILLINOIS

THE GRADUATE SCHOOL

June 3, 1911

I HEREBY RECOMMEND THAT THE THESIS PREPARED UNDER MY SUPERVISION BY

Truman Lee Kelley.

ENTITLED Correlation Between Certain Mental Capacities

BE ACCEPTED AS FULFILLING THIS PART OF THE REQUIREMENTS FOR THE

DEGREE OF Master of Arts in Psychology

A H Sutherland
In Charge of Major Work

Stephen S. Colvin
Head of Department

Recommendation concurred in:

Committee
on
Final Examination

197660

INTRODUCTION.

The problem of the interdependence of human capacities is a very old one, but only in recent years has it been approached from a standpoint other than that of mere opinion, based upon "common observation". Some of the conclusions which were drawn from general observation, unchecked by measurement and statistical investigation, have been erroneous. The following serve as illustrations; the idea that ability in the logical thot processes is inversely correlated with ability to deal with concrete material, or the mechanical arts; the idea that physical strength and general athletic ability is inversely correlated with mental ability. Illustrations of such general incorrect notions might be multiplied. Since 1890 it has been realized that these questions can be taken outside of the realm of opinion and placed in that of more or less definitely established fact by scientific method. Two investigations, one conducted by W. C. Bagley at Wisconsin in 1897 and the other by Cyril Burt at Oxford in 1909, will serve as types of the pioneer and of the modern studies along these lines. The former study# deals with the correlation between mental and motor ability. Dynamometer tests, motor coordination tests, trilling tests, etc. were used to measure motor ability and teachers' estimates and reaction times were the basis for the mental tests. One conclusion, now considered erroneous, drawn from this experiment is that an inverse correlation exists between mental and motor ability. The mathematical treatment of the data obtained was by unrefined methods and the conclusions, as illustrated have been largely displaced by later investigations, but on the whole the problem was approached in the right spirit and this inves-

American Journal of Psychology, v.12, pp.193ff.

tigation takes a place among those marking a new era in the study of such problems.

The study by Burt# attempts to establish the correlation between imputed general intelligence, as determined by the head masters' estimates, and ability to learn, to discriminate, to make certain motor coordinations, etc., as determined by variously devised psychological tests. His conclusions are quite in harmony with extensive investigations conducted by others during the last decade. From the results of Burt and of others the following generalizations are drawn, tho it is difficult to generalize from experiments conducted under such varying conditions:: (1) There is no positive correlation (at least not greater than that represented by a Pearson coefficient of correlation of .10) between any trait making for human and individual welfare and a trait opposed to it. It is, of course, possible that investigation of traits not yet studied may reveal such a correlation. This principle is one of the most valuable and fundamental to which the study of correlation has led and it is sufficiently well established to warrant being taken as a permanent mile-post. (2) The correlation between anthropometric measurements and mental tests is very small. (3) The correlation between various motor and mental abilities varies between .00 and .50 (in terms of a Pearson coefficient). (4) The correlation between sensory discrimination and tests of intelligence varies between .25 and .75. (5) The correlation between different tests measuring intelligence varies between .40 and .90.

The present investigation deals with the correlation of certain laboratory tests in discrimination, reaction time and association

---

British Journal of Psychology, December 1909.

with class standings in mathematics, science, and foreign languages, as determined by the class records of the students.

UPPER AND LOWER LIMENS OF AUDITION.

Tests of the upper and lower limens of audition were planned for the purposes of this experiment. The instrument used to find the upper limen was the Galton whistle and that for the lower limen the Appun lamella. It was found after considerable experimenting that neither of these tests could be conducted with sufficient accuracy to warrant their use.

The difficulty which arose in connection with the upper limen was unexpected. The limen could be determined with very considerable precision at any one sitting, but when the experiment was repeated some days later the limen, in most cases, was found to be just as definitely in some other place, several thousand vibrations a second away from the previous determination. The general tendency was for the limen to rise. This change seemed to be practically independent of physical conditions and very largely a matter of training. An extreme case illustrating this progressive change of the upper limen is that of the experimentor who took the readings on the Galton whistle for the observors. At the beginning of these observations he was able to hear a sound of 28,000 vibrations a second. Observations were taken at intervals for a month and he noted that his limen was continually rising. At the end of the month he was able to hear as a tone vibrations of the rate of 40,000 per second. Nor was his case unique, except in degree. Second and sometimes third observations were taken on a number of the subjects, showing such increases as the following; from 28,900 to 39,000; from 29,700 to 38,000; from 27,100 to 28,830; from 34,710 to 36,600; etc. The upper limen

seemed to be a very well defined point at the time when tested, but its instability rendered it inaccurate for correlation purposes.

The Appun lamella proved a very unsatisfactory instrument for determining the lower limen because of the unavoidable sound in starting it, but this was not the only difficulty involved. Many of the observors felt that the low sound turned into a flutter by imperceptible degrees and to say that the limen is at a particular point does not represent a fact in consciousness. There seems to be considerable ground for justification of this since the difficulty was experienced by more than a majority of the observors. One observor, who thot that he could discern a limen, was equally sure that, by altering his attention he could change the limen; i.e. by one attitude toward any of the vibrations lying between 22 and 17 a second he could hear them as a smooth tone and by another attitude, he could hear them as a flutter. For these reasons this experiment was discarded.

DISCRIMINATION OF GREYS.

The object of this test was to obtain individual measures of the ability to discriminate greys. The procedure was as follows: A Marbe color mixer was used. In its center was an unchanging disk of 2.5 cm. diameter, composed of 183 degrees of white paper and 177 degrees of black (Milton Bradley standard white and black used thruout). Outside of this was a disk of 7.7 cm. diameter, composed of black and white papers of the same make, in a proportion which varied according to the setting of the instrument. This color mixer was set up in a dark room in front of an opening in a black cardboard box, as shown by the cross section sketch on the following page. "M" is the disk of the color mixer, directly in front of the opening "J" of the same

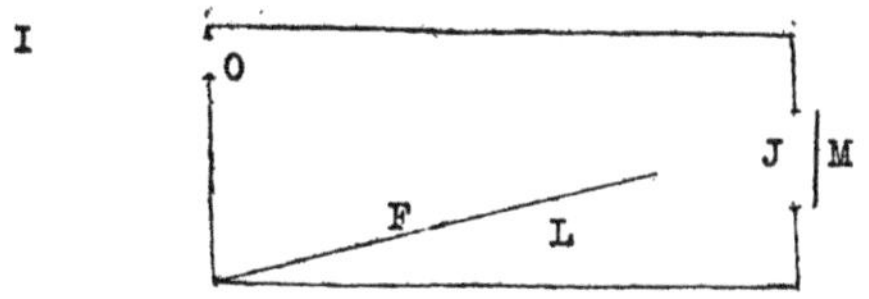

size as the disk "M". The observor "I" looks thru the opening "O" upon the disk "M". The illumination is by means of a lamp situated at "L", so that light falls upon "M", but is screened from the observor by the flap "F". Everything about the box is made of black cardboard. Its dimensions are 45 cm. in length by 18 x 18 cm. The source of illumination was a 55 candle power ground glass incandescant light, run on a fairly constant 220 volt alternating circuit, and situated 8 cm. below and 15 cm. in front of the disk on the color mixer. The observor's eyes were approximately 75 cm. in front of and 25 cm. above the center of the disk. Preliminary experiments established the fact that when the proportions of black and white in the outside disk were such as was represented by a reading of 12 on the scale the outside and inside disks appeared to be a match for all observors. Measurement showed that the outside disk was then composed of 203 degrees of white and 157 degrees of black. The procedure was to start with this match and increase or decrease the proportion of white, while the observor was watching, to such a point that the outside disk appeared "too light" or "too dark" to be a match with the inside disk. 25 such observations were taken, twelve being "too dark" readings and eleven "too light" readings. Observations were discontinued when after images appeared or when the eyes were fatigued. The starting point - scale reading of 12 - was found as indicated rather than by measuring the number of degrees of white and black in the outside disk to correspond to the number in the inside disk, 183 degrees of white and 177 degrees of black, for the reason that the

latter method would not have taken account of the effect continually present because of the black background. The following table gives the results abtained by the different observors A, B, C, etc.

Observor	Dark readings	Light readings	Match	Average dis.dif.	Average var'n
A	15.48	10.41	12.94	2.53	.38
B	15.66	9.78	12.72	2.94	.82
C	13.75	9.87	11.81	1.94	.28
D	13.80	9.73	11.77	2.03	.31
E	15.13	8.24	11.68	3.45	.45
F	14.28	8.32	11.30	2.97	.60
G	13.90	10.78	12.34	1.56	.36
H	14.27	10.88	12.58	1.69	.18
I					
J	14.37	8.90	11.64	2.73	.29
K	15.83	8.50	12.16	3.67	.63
L	14.96	10.96	12.96	2.00	.26

The first column gives the average reading at which the outside disk first appeared darker than the inside disk and the second column gives a similar average for the readings at which the outside disk appeared lighter than the inside disk. The third column is the average of the first and second and is given as the reading at which the two disks most exactly match. The fourth column gives the "average discrimination difference" and is the average of the divergences of the individual readings from this best match reading. The last column, giving the "average variation" is the average of the divergences of the individual readings from the average "too dark" (column 1) and the average "too light" (column 2) readings, as the case may be.

These results give the following two sets of measures which will be used later; (1) the measures for the average discrimination difference; and (2) the measures for the average variation.

ASSOCIATION EXPERIMENT.

This test is a free association experiment and the method is somewhat more complete than the ordinary free association experiment in that complete introspections are recorded.

The following 100 words were used as stimulus words:

1 arch	34 ghostly	67 consent
2 prude	35 future	68 courage
3 egotism	36 text	69 cowardice
4 single	37 success	70 course
5 chastity	38 abstract	71 habit
6 ginger	39 fatalism	72 gamble
7 shrew	40 gauze	73 purity
8 adapt	41 error	74 drug
9 tough	42 gargle	75 snake
10 morality	43 energetic	76 intention
11 rubber	44 apathy	77 caution
12 coquet	45 silk	78 alimony
13 kick	46 stage	79 atheism
14 forward	47 curse	80 cuckoo
15 truth	48 duty	81 height
16 cake	49 valor	82 deject
17 skeptic	50 velvet	83 concept
18 extort	51 secure	84 temperance
19 modest	52 giggle	85 chide
20 religion	53 inhuman	86 law
21 knife	54 ecstacy	87 virtue
22 fanatic	55 lace	88 reverse
23 insult	56 hint	89 handsome
24 flaxen	57 blush	90 temper
25 soul	58 wicked	91 heaven
26 bar	59 conscience	92 quitter
27 president	60 shoulder	93 thrill
28 fluster	61 graft	94 character
29 juicy	62 behave	95 thief
30 death	63 sacrifice	96 guile
31 press	64 philosophy	97 bully
32 beauty	65 trifle	98 revel
33 retard	66 bedlam	99 revenge
		100 iniquity

It will be noticed that a very generous proportion of them are more or less abstract in their nature. These abstract words were chosen with the aim of bringing out significant modes of reaction,

which it was thot they would accomplish more readily than concrete and less difficult words. The remainder are intended to represent a random sampling of the words used in ordinary life.

The instructions to the observors were that upon hearing one of these stimulus words they were to react with the first word that came to mind. They were told that no logical relation between stimulus word and reaction word was demanded - the only requirement being that the reaction word must be one suggested in some manner by the stimulus word.

The time between stimulus word and reaction was measured by means of a stop watch, operated by the experimentor. The watch was read to 10'ths of a second by estimation between 5'ths of a second divisions and was started and stopped by the armature of an electric magnet which was in circuit with an easily operated key. This arrangement proved more precise than could be obtained by manipulating the watch directly. A series of tests to determine the probable error in the time of observation due to the experimentor's manipulation showed it to be about .1 second, i.e. his average variability in measuring a stimulus of known duration was a little less than .1 second. The time between end of stimulus word and beginning of reaction word is taken.

After the reaction the observor was asked for a complete introspection concerning the association process and a shorthand record of this account is recorded. (The entire data for this experiment is given in the appendix.) The data is classified according to three schemes. (The complete classification follows the data in the appendix.)

(1) All the associations which the introspections showed re-

ferred to some particular situation are classed in a Particular Situation class. All other associations are put into a General Situation class. The reference to a particular situation is shown by the visual imagery or other thot process being a memory of some specific circumstance. The following are illustrations of this class:: Observor E #5 (See record in the appendix) - stimulus "chastity", reaction "pure", introspection "I thot of one of Shakespere's plays. The class discussed the characters of the play and the purity of the heroine. Visual image of the page in the book dealing with this." Another illustration: Observor I #23 - stimulus "insult", reaction "offence", introspection "The idea came from having recently heard Ex-governor Glenn, who spoke about the insult to the white population. He seemed to pronounce the word as tho it were 'insu-u-lt'."

(2) The data is classified according to the imagery involved, using the following subdivisions: Articulatory; Visual; Kinesthetic; a general group composed of Olfactory, Gustatory, Cutaneous, Auditory and Organic; 2'd Articulatory (by which is meant that the reaction word is one that had occurred at least once before in the series); 2'd Visual (by which is meant that the visual imagery is the same as that called up by some preceding word); No Imagery. In a very considerable number of observations more than one kind of imagery was involved and in such cases as many different kinds of imagery were credited with the reaction as the introspection showed to be present. The reliability of these different classes differs greatly: The first class, Articulatory imagery, is very unreliable for the reason that most of the observors, altho advanced students of psychology, were uncertain as to the criteria of articulatory imagery. This was equally true of kinesthetic, olfactory, gustatory, cutaneous, auditory

and organic imagery. It is not the case with visual imagery - the introspections are definite and in only a few cases does the observor show doubt as to the existence or non existence of visual imagery. The 2'd Articulatory class is exact, depending entirely upon the previous use of the reaction word. In explaining his introspections the observor very generally used the stimulus word and necessarily thot it in all cases. For this reason, in later reactions, if the reaction word previously occurred as a stimulus word the association was classed under 2'd Articulatory. The 2'd Visual class proved so small that it need not be considered. The No Imagery class is a small one, comprising only those reactions in which the observor definitely said there was no imagery. If the introspection contains no statement at all in regard to the imagery the association is put into the Articulatory class, thus further tending to make the class unreliable. The only two classes considered accurate for the purposes of this study are the Visual and 2'd Articulatory.

(3) A classification according to the nature of the mental process involved in association is used. It is a modification of the classification used by Wells# and consists of the following classes: (1) Sound; (2) Phrase Completion; (3) Synonyms; (4) Contrast; (5) Coexistence; (6) Predicate and Judgment of Quality; (7) Subordination; (8) Coordination; (9) Supraordination; (10) Egocentric; (11) Egocentric Predicate; (12) Subject Relation; (13) Object Relation; (14) Causality; (15) Failure. An explanation in some detail will be necessary to indicate just what is put into each class and the lines of demarcation between the classes. The classification is a purely arbitrary one and there is no natural line of division between classes,

American Journal of Psychology, January 1909.

but that fact does not in itself destroy the usefulness of the classification if it is possible to measure the degree of relation between the classes and thus utilize their interdependence. A further discussion of this point is given later in describing the method of grouping. The following principles are followed in the classification of the data:

(1) Class 1 comprises those associations in which the sound of the word played the leading part, as in the following: Observor D #49, stimulus "valor", reaction "vanity", introspection "A sound reaction. After reacting the meaning came as 'bravery'." Associations in which the reaction word is some modified form of the stimulus word are also found in this class, e.g. Observor D #64, stimulus "philosophy", reaction "philosopher". There is little difficulty in determining the associations which belong in this class, tho occasionally an uncertainty arises, e.g. stimulus "man", reaction "mankind" might properly be either in this class, the class Supraordination, or the class Phrase Completion. This difficulty is not serious as the introspections almost invariably indicate to which class such a reaction belongs. The difficulty in distinguishing between class 2 and class 1 is slightly greater than that between any of the other classes and class 1.

(2) Class 2 is comprised of those reactions in which a word (in case the stimulus is the first part of a compound word), a phrase, or an idea, is completed by the addition of another word or words. Such a reaction as the following; stimulus "text", reaction "textbook" is put into this class, tho it does not differ much from the following; stimulus "man", reaction "mankind", which would have been put into class 1. Another illustration of a reaction put into this

class is the following; stimulus "shrew", reaction "Taming of the Shrew", introspection "I thot of the play 'Taming of the Shrew' in articulatory terms." This class is not as clearly defined as the first, conflicting more or less with most of the other classes. Illustrations of the conflict with the different classes are readily available - the following is one; stimulus "black", reaction "white", introspection "I thot of the phrase 'black and white'." Whether this belongs here or in Contrast is a question. If the phrase were "black and blue" it would have been put into this class. The Phrase Completion class especially competed with the Subject Relation and Object Relation classes in its claim for certain reactions, e.g. observor D #88, stimulus "reverse", reaction "engine", introspection "Clear visual image of the throttle of an engine." This quite clearly belongs in the Object Relation class, but if the introspection had been "I thot of the phrase 'reverse the engine'", the reaction would have belonged in the Phrase Completion class. In a number of cases the introspections do not clear up the difficulty. It is felt by the writer that the distinction between the Phrase Completion class and the Subject Relation and Object Relation classes is particularly indefinite.

(3) The Synonym class is composed of those cases in which the reaction word is more or less accurately a synonym of the stimulus word. The Identity, or Synonym, class gradually grades into the Coexistence class or the Coordination class. However, if a word might equally well be put into the Coexistence or Synonym class, it was always put into the latter.

(4) The Contrast class is composed of those reactions showing contrast between stimulus and reaction word, and also of certain re-

actions in which the introspection shows plainly that the idea of contrast is present, tho the stimulus and reaction words do not show it, e.g. observor I #69, stimulus "cowardice", reaction "fight", the introspection giving as the idea, that the opposite of cowardice - courage - can be shown only by a fight. As the idea of contrast between stimulus and reaction is less and less pronounced this class grades imperceptibly into the class Coordination. It is also related to Coexistence since a large number of contrasting ideas are also coexisting. If the contrast is not a perfect one there may be a question whether the association belongs in the Contrast or one of the classes Subordination, Supraordination. This latter difficulty did not prove a very general one.

(5) The Coexistence class is a very general class. It is related to all the other classes, tho it was not credited with any reaction that could be put into any other one. When the reaction word is quite apparently related in some way to the stimulus word, but in so obscure a way that it cannot be said to be a relation of Identity, Contrast, etc. the association is classified here. In certain of the reactions of this class the stimulus and reaction words represent things which coexist in nature, and in certain others the stimulus and reaction words represent two ideas which coexist only in the realm of thot.

(6) In the beginning of the classification it was attempted to distinguish between a simple predicate and a judgment of quality, but the two classes so nearly approached identity in the mind of the classifier that it was abandoned and in the following discussion the two classes are grouped as a single Predicate class. There are two main types of association in this class; (a) those in which some ob-

ject is named as the stimulus and a predicate of it given as the reaction word, and (b) those in which a predicate is named and some object given to which this predicate is appropriate. A reaction such as the following would be put into this class; stimulus "beauty", reaction "girl". It is thot that such a stimulus is taken either as "beautiful" or immediately suggests it, making the association of the genuine predicate type.

(7) and (9) The classes Subordination and Supraordination are difficult classes to separate since a reaction such as the following; stimulus "horse", reaction "animal" may be looked upon in one of two ways, either (a) that the observor thot of "horse" and then the larger group to which it belonged, or (b) that the observor had a number of general ideas within easy reach and in searching for examples "horse" came as an illustration of the general class "animal". In making a distinction between these two classes, if the introspection does not reveal to which class the association belongs, reactions such as that cited are put into the Supraordination class. The Predicate and Subordination classes are related since the mental process of attaching a specific example to a larger class is quite analogous to that of attaching a predicate to an object. For a similar reason the Predicate and Supraordination classes are related.

(8) The Coordination class is arbitrarily limited to cases in which the stimulus word and reaction word are of equal logical value, unless the introspection shows in some other case that the coordination idea is present, e.g. it is of course quite possible that the idea of coordination may be present when stimulus and reaction words are as different as the following; stimulus "beauty", reaction "man"- in such a case the introspection might reveal that the idea was of a

"beautiful woman" and a "handsome man". The relation between Coordination and Synonyms, and Contrast, has been discussed under those topics.

(10) and (11) The class Egocentric contains only eight observations and the class Egocentric Predicate contains none at all, hence the discussion of these classes will be omitted. It is quite possible that they might be of very considerable size with different observors.

(12) and (13) The Subject Relation class is comprised of two kinds of reactions; (a) those in which the stimulus word is a verb and the reaction word the subject of it, and (b) those in which the stimulus word is a noun, conceived of as the subject of the reaction word, which is a verb. Similarly there are two kinds of reactions put into the Object Relation class. The similarity between these classes and the Phrase Completion class has already been noted. The number of observations in these two classes is small.

(14) Causality is a very limited class and comprises those reactions in which the stimulus represents the cause of the reaction word, or vice versa. The following is an illustration; observor F #23, stimulus "insult". reaction "man", introspection "Hazy visual image of a man coming along the sidewalk and shoving a lady over to one side". The illustration cited shows the close connection between this class and the Subject Relation and Object Relation classes.

(15) The Failure class is composed of two kinds of reactions; (a) those in which there is a blocking of the association processes and a corresponding inability to react, and (b) those in which the reaction, tho set off by the stimulus word, has no connection with it and is, in reality, a reaction to an ideational process inaugurated

by the observor entirely independent of the stimulus word. Very few reactions of this nature occurred, and in fact the entire class is small.

Following is a table showing the more important elements of the complete classification given in the appendix:

Observors	Reaction Time	Variability	Particular Sit.	Visual Imagery	2'd Articulatory
A	1.4	.30	20	74	16
B	1.0	.20	43	70	6
C	1.3	.50	6	5	3
D	1.45	.90	5	33	3
E	1.7	.45	49	57	8
F	1.4	.30	9	38	9
G	1.2	.30	30	71	7
H	1.3	.30	4	41	7
I	1.4	.335	49	48	3
J	1.25	.35	6	62	13
K	1.0	.235	8	82	43
L	1.7	.50	22	56	4

	S'nd	Phrase Comp.	Synonyms	Contrast	Coex.	Pred.	Subor.	Coor.	Supra.	Egoc.	Subj. Rel.	Obj. Rel.	Causal.	Failure	
A	4	9	21	2	11	36	8	4	0	4	1	0	0	0	A
B	2	14	4	3	14	43	5	6	6	0	1	1	1	0	B
C	1	15	49	0	9	14	3	0	1	0	1	0	3	4	C
D	36	9	19	4	5	8	3	3	2	0	0	1	0	10	D
E	12	8	11	2	17	24	4	5	5	0	3	5	2	2	E
F	2	28	25	11	11	10	1	3	1	0	2	1	4	1	F
G	3	8	22	1	23	18	14	0	0	0	2	3	5	1	G
H	3	9	28	5	12	18	5	3	1	3	3	3	4	3	H
I	6	6	33	13	12	5	3	8	5	0	0	3	2	4	I
J	2	7	31	16	5	12	2	12	1	0	1	2	4	5	J
K	4	12	3	1	12	30	2	2	10	0	8	9	3	4	K
L	7	17	14	4	12	16	4	6	5	1	5	3	5	1	L
	82	142	260	62	143	234	54	52	37	8	27	31	33	35	

In this table the measure of the reaction time, appearing in the second column, is the median. One-half the difference between the upper and lower quartiles is given as the measure of variability. In the remaining columns the figures given indicate the number of reactions put into these classes.

REACTION TIME MEASURES.

The use of the median instead of the average as the best measure for the reaction time is based upon the fact that there is a skew distribution of reaction times, represented by a curve such as the following:

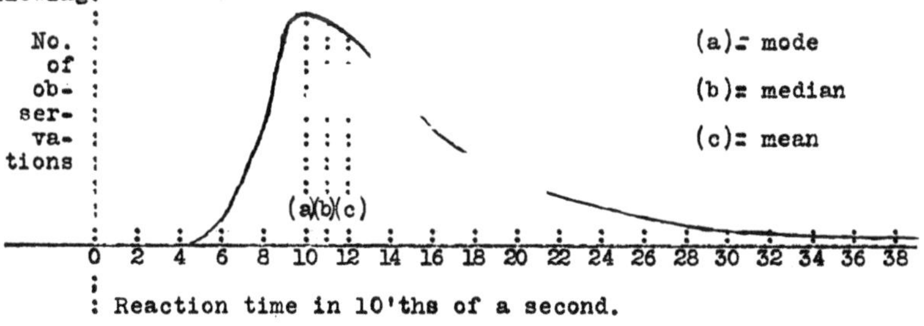

The mode and the mean are on opposite sides of the median, the mode being closer to the short time reaction end and the mean closer to the long time reaction end of the distribution curve. One factor tending toward such a skew distribution lies in the existence of a number of reactions in which there is a blocking or conflict in the mental process, thus excessively lengthening the reaction time. If this factor could be entirely eliminated it is still probable that there would be a skew distribution since there is an absolute lower limit, less than which the reaction time cannot be, but no such upper limit. With such a skew distribution the average is too greatly affected by a few large observations to make it a desirable measure of

reaction time. Again, the mode takes no account whatsoever of any measures except those neighboring to it and is therefore not a desirable measure. The median is affected to an equal extent by every measure, large or small, and is here considered the best single value to measure the reaction time of the individual. The same objection that applies to the average applies to such measures as the mean deviation, or the standard deviation, as measures of variability, and for the same reason that the median is chosen as the best measure of reaction time, the difference in time between the upper and lower quartiles is chosen as a measure of variability. One-half this difference is equal to the median deviation of the observations, measured from a point very near the median.

GROUPING OF CLASSES.

In the classification according to the nature of the mental process involved there are fifteen classes, with varying numbers of observations in each. In order to have measures of the types of reaction which are more reliable than is possible under such conditions certain of these classes have been combined into groups. There are two methods for determining the classes which shall be so combined.

(1) The combination of the classes into groups according to the judgment of the classifier. According to this method his idea as to the intimacy of the classes would be the sole justification for combining them. Instead of adopting such a classification, which would be simply an a priori judgment on the part of the classifier, the following method is used:

(2) The degree to which two classes are correlated as to frequency of occurrence is made the basis for grouping. Without assuming a similarity of mental process involved in reacting according to

the different classes so grouped, a high correlation would indicate that a tendency to react according to one of these classes is accompanied by a pronounced tendency to react according to the other classes in the group. The following table shows the correlation existing between each class and certain of the other classes:

	Sound	Phrase Comp.	Synonyms	Con-	Coex.	Pred.	Subor.	Coor.	Supra.	Causal.	Subj. Rel.	Obj. Rel.
Sound	1.											
Phrase Comp.	-.28	1.										
Synonyms	-.75	-.37	1.									
Contrast			.44	1.								
Coexist.	S	S	-.37		1.							
Predicate	S	S	-.55		.60	1.						
Subor.	S	S	S		.55	.55	1.					
Coor.	S	S	.09	.69	.09	S	S	1.				
Supra.	.31	S	-.69		S	.25	-.25	S	1.			
Causality	-.34						S		-.55	1.		
Subj. Rel.							S		.28	.47	1.	
Obj. Rel.										.28	.52	1.

For the method of calculating these coefficients of correlation and their probable error see page 25. In any square in the table the coefficient of correlation found is that between the classes indicated at the top of the column and the left of the row in which the coefficient occurs. Where there are blank spaces in the table coefficients of correlation were not calculated, but the data was carefully inspected and it is known that no appreciable positive correlations occur. Those squares containing an "S" indicate that the cor-

relation is small, in fact in no case appreciably larger than the probable error, which is .19. An inspection of this table shows that certain classes may be combined into groups on the basis of high correlation between them.

(Alpha) Synonyms, Coordination and Contrast are combined into a single group, Alpha, on account of the following correlations: Between Synonyms and Contrast, .44; between Contrast and Coordination, 69. The positive correlation between Synonyms and Coordination, 09, is so small as to be no additional reason for the grouping.

(Beta) Object Relation, Subject Relation and Causality are combined into a single group, Beta, on the basis of the following correlations; between Object Relation and Subject Relation,.62; between Subject Relation and Causality, .47; and between Causality and Object Relation, .28.

(Gamma) Predicates, Subordination and Coexistence are combined into a single group, Gamma, on the basis of the following correlations: between Predicates and Coexistence, .60; between Coexistence and Subordination, .55; and between Subordination and Predicates, .55.

The following classes show no marked positive correlations, i.e. correlations greater than twice the probable error: Sound, Phrase Completion, Supraordination, Failure, and accordingly they are not grouped.

The positive correlation coefficients here given are somewhat too small and the negative coefficients too large for the reason that there is a tendency toward negative correlation, since the more in one class the less number that remain which can be put into another class. After a reaction is put into one class there is less probability, in the ratio of 99 to 100, of any other class containing as great a num-

ber as it otherwise would. For this reason the importance of negative correlation coefficients lies in their ability to indicate which classes are most strongly opposed, rather than to accurately measure the amount of apposition.

Following is a table giving the number of times the observors reacted according to the Alpha, Beta and Gamma types:

	Alpha	Beta	Gamma
A	27	1	55
B	13	3	62
C	49	4	26
D	26	1	16
E	18	10	45
F	39	7	22
G	23	10	55
H	36	10	35
I	54	5	20
J	59	7	19
K	6	20	44
L	24	13	32

This table is obtained by combining the appropriate columns of the table on page 16.

THE OBSERVORS.

The observors are all men with the exception of observor C. Observors A. B. C. D. F. G and H are either graduate students or have completed work for a Ph.D. degree. The others are all advanced undergraduates. Observor E is a Japanese student who has a good command of the English language. Observor I is a Russian and a lin-

quist of very exceptional ability. He is gifted with a remarkable memory and is also exceptionally strong in mathematics, engineering, science and economics. Observor H is a keen student of philosophy and his grades in other subjects are perhaps considerably below his ability in them. This is probably the case also with some of the other observors. For reasons mentioned in the next paragraph the rankings in Mathematics, Science and Foreign Languages do not conform exactly with the grades received in these subjects, however, the rankings given represent grades and are indicative of ability only in so far as are the grades received.

RANKINGS IN MATHEMATICS, SCIENCE AND FOREIGN LANGUAGES.

Mathematics, Science and Foreign Languages are chosen because grades in these subjects are more accessible than is true of subjects less universally pursued. The grades recorded in the following table are taken from the registrar's records when possible. If the student's undergraduate work was done at some other institution equivalent grades at the University of Illinois are recorded. In some cases this has involved an estimate, which has been based upon the student's own judgment of his ability and upon other available information in regard to equivalent grades. Following is a table of grades and rankings. A star indicates a change in the order of ranking from that of grading.

	Mathematics		Science		Foreign lang.	
	Grade	Rank	Grade	Rank	Grade	Rank
A	91	1#	91	4	87	6
B	81	7	88	6.5	94	2.5
C	93	3	94.2	3	94	2.5
D	88	5	95	2	84	8
E	83	6	88	6.5	89	4
F	90	4	93	1#	86.5	7
G	73	11.5	77	11	85	5#
H	73	11.5	80	10	83	9
I	84	2#	86.5	5#	98	1
J	80	9	85.7	8	69	12
K	80	9	76.5	12	72.5	11
L	80	9	82.2	9	77	10

In every case where the order of ranking has been changed from that of grading and an observor with a lower grade in a subject ranked ahead of some with higher grades the change is amply justified because the lower grades are averages of grades received, in whole or in large part, in advanced courses and the grades of the observors passed were received in more or less elementary courses. To illustrate - observor I with a grade of 84 in Mathematics is ranked second, ahead of observors C and F, but not ahead of observor A. I's grade is for advanced work in Mathematics, as also is A's, but C's and F's grades are for elementary mathematics. It is the opinion of the writer that the ranking as given corresponds very closely with the ranking of these observors if determined according to grades received in identical courses in Mathematics, Science and Foreign Languages, but it is not thot that such grades would represent very accurately the abilities of the students in the subjects named for the reason that certain of them would make little effort to rank well according to grade. For example; G and H both receive grades around 95 in subjects which interest them and which they spend their time upon, and if ability in Mathematics could be measured it is hardly likely that they would stand last.

TABLES.

The following table gives rankings in all the preceding tests. Observor I did not take the discrimination of greys test. The abbreviations at the head of the table have meanings as follows: Mathematics; Science; Foreign Languages; Average discrimination difference in the discrimination of greys test; Average variation in the discrimination of greys test; (the remaining measures refer to the association experiment) Median time of reaction; Variability in reac-

tion time, i.e. the semi-quartile difference; Recall of a Particular Situation; Visual imagery; 2'd Articulatory imagery, i.e. repetition in the use of reaction words; Alpha group; Beta group; Gamma group, as defined on page 20.

TABLE OF RANKINGS.

	Scholarship			Greys test		Association test							
	Math.	Sci.	F.L.	D.D.	Var.	Time	Var.	Part. Sit.	Vis.	2'd Art.	Alpha	Beta	Gamma
A	1	4	6	6	7	8	4.5	4.5	2	2	6	11.5	2.5
B	7	6.5	2.5	8	11	1.5	1	3	4	8	11	10	1
C	3	3	2.5	3	3	5.5	10.5	9.5	12	11	3	9	8
D	5	2	8	5	5	10	12	11	11	11	7	11.5	12
E	6	6.5	4	10	8	11.5	9	1.5	6	5	10	4	4
F	4	1	7	9	9	8	4.5	7	10	4	4	6.5	9
G	11.5	11	5	1	6	3	4.5	4.5	3	6.5	9	4	2.5
H	11.5	10	9	2	1	5.5	4.5	12	9	6.5	5	4	6
I	2	5	1			8	7	1.5	8	11	2	8	10
J	9	8	12	7	4	4	8	9.5	5	3	1	6.5	11
K	9	12	11	11	10	1.5	2	8	1	1	12	1	5
L	9	9	10	4	2	11.5	10.5	6	7	9	8	2	7

Following is a table of coefficients of correlation, calculated from the rankings in the preceding table:

TABLE OF COEFFICIENTS OF CORRELATION.

	Scholarship: Math.	Sci.	F. L.	Greys test: D.D.	Var.	Association test: Time	Var.	Part. Sit.	Vis.	2'd Art.	Alpha	Beta	G'ma
Math.	1.												
Sci.	.81	1.											
F.L.	.44	.31	1.										
Greys D.D.	-.34	.00	.00	1.									
Var.	-.26	-.07	-.41	.76	1.								
Ass'n Time	-.28	-.47	.00	.00	.00	1.							
Var.	.05	-.34	.00	-.28	-.74	.65	1.						
Part. Sit.	.25	.00	.60			.16	.28	1.					
Vis.	-.31	-.71	-.05			.47	.52	.22	1.				
2'd Art.	.00	-.34	-.44			.22	.52	.00	.48	1.			
Alpha	.37	.37	.19	.38	.52	-.22	-.28	-.34	-.50	-.22	1.		
Beta	-.55	-.75	-.44	.00	.03	.22	.31	.00	.34	.37	-.31	1.	
Gamma	-.22	.28	.22	-.07	-.43	.34	.55	.47	.65	.34	-.65	.22	1.

In any square the coefficient of correlation given is that between the subjects indicated at the top of the column and the left of the row in which the coefficient occurs. These coefficients are comparable with Pearson coefficients of correlation, but were not calculated according to the Pearson method. Spearman R-coefficients of correlation were calculated and transferred approximately into Pearson r-coefficients by means of the relation $r = \sin(R \frac{Pi}{2})$.

Assuming that there is no correlation known to exist the probable error of these coefficients is as follows:

$P.E._r = 1.5\ P.E._R = 1.5(.43/\sqrt{n}) = 1.5(.43/\sqrt{12}) = .19.$

If the correlation coefficient is as high as .40 we may believe that

there is some correlation and use for the probable error $(1-r^2)$ times the probable error found above, or $(1 - r^2).19$.

For the vacant squares no coefficients of correlation were calculated, being considered of no material value.

INTERPRETATION AND CONCLUSIONS.

The small numbers of individuals studied renders the results inconclusive, tho they are considered to suggest the probable results of more extensive investigation. The reliability of these results is measured by the probable error of the coefficients of correlation. To illustrate; the correlation coefficient between F.L. and Part.Sit. found in the table is .60. The chances are 1 to 1 that this correlation coefficient is in error by an amount as great as .12 $\{(1-.60^2) \times .19 = .12\}$. The probability that it is in error by an amount as great as .24 is 1 to 4.6; the probability that it is in error by an amount as great as .36 is 1 to 22; the probability that it is in error by an amount as great as .48 is 1 to 143; and the probability that it is in error by an amount as great as .60, or that the correlation does not exist, is 1 to 1341. Credence can therefore be given to the existence of a correlation between Foreign Languages and the recall of a particular situation in the association experiment, but the exact size of this correlation is not determined by this data. If we consider a smaller coefficient of correlation, e.g. that between Math. and Part. Sit., $r = .25$, the chances are 1 to 1 that this coefficient of correlation is in error by an amount as great as .19 $\{(1 - .25^2).19 = .18$, but since r is so small we are hardly justified in using this formula, tho if we should use it the difference would be only that between .18 and .19$\}$, and the chances are 1 to 1.6 that there is no correlation. Conclusions, therefore, can-

not be drawn from such a correlation coefficient and in the following work significance will be given particularly to coefficients of correlation greater than .40, at which point the chances are 1 to 10 that at least some correlation does exist.

Following is a restatement of the table on page 25 arranging subjects in the order of magnitude in which they are correlated with Mathematics, Foreign languages, etc.

MATHEMATICS		SCIENCE		FOREIGN LANGUAGES	
Sci.	.81	Math.	.81	Part. Sit.	.60
F.L.	.44	Alpha	.37	Math.	.44
Alpha	.37	F.L.	.31	Sci.	.31
Part. Sit.	.25	Gamma	.28	Gamma	.22
Ass'n Var.	.05	Part. Sit.	.00	Alpha	.19
2'd Art.	.00	Grey D.D.	.00	Ass'n Time	.00
Gamma	-.22	Grey Var.	-.07	Ass'n Var.	.00
Grey Var.	-.26	Ass'n Var.	-.34	Grey D.D.	.00
Ass'n Time	-.28	2'd Art.	-.34	Vis.	-.05
Grey D.D.	-.34	Ass'n Time	-.47	Grey Var.	-.41
Vis.	-.31	Vis.	-.71	2'd Art.	-.44
Beta	-.55	Beta	-.75	Beta	-.44

ASS'N-TIME		ASS'N-VAR.		GREY-DIS.DIF.		GREY-VAR.	
Gamma	.34	Gamma	.55	Alpha	.38	Alpha	.52
Beta	.22	Beta	.31	Ass'n Time	.00	Beta	.03
Grey D.D.	.00	Grey D.D.	-.28	Beta	.00	Ass'n Time	.00
Grey Var.	.00	Alpha	-.28	Gamma	-.07	Gamma	-.43
Alpha	-.22	Grey Var.	-.74	Ass'n Var.	-.28	Ass'n Var.	-.74

An inspections of the columns for Mathematics, Science and Foreign Languages reveals the following facts:

(1) The recall of a particular situation shows a positive correlation of .25 with Mathematics and .60 with Foreign Languages.

(2) The variability in association time is not materially correlated with these subjects.

(3) The time of reaction in the association experiment is not in general pronouncedly correlated, tho being negatively correlated to an appreciable degree with Science.

(4) The ability to discriminate greys is not materially correlated.

(5) The variability in the discrimination of greys shows slightly more negative correlation than the ability to discriminate greys, tho the correlation is not pronounced.

(6) Repetition in reaction words shows a slight negative correlation, especially to Foreign Languages.

(7) Visual imagery is negatively correlated, especially to Science.

(8) The group Alpha, (Synonyms, Coordination and Contrast), is favorably correlated with Mathematics, Science and Foreign Languages.

(9) The Gamma group, (Predicates, Coexistence, and Subordination), is not materially correlated with these scholastic subjects.

(10) The Beta group, (Subject Relation, Object Relation and Causality), shows a pronounced negative correlation with all three subjects.

Referring to the test in Discrimination of Greys, we find:

(11) That every subject, except Ass'n Time, which shows correlation with the ability to discriminate greys shows a higher correlation with the variability in the discrimination of greys.

(12) That there is a high negative correlation between the variability in the discrimination of greys and the variability in the time of reaction in the association experiment.

Referring to the Association test, we find:

(13) That the variability in the time of reaction is more high-

ly correlated than the time of reaction itself.

The reason for the existence of the tendencies noted is largely a matter of conjecture and the following are given as theories of explanation:

(1) The recall of a particular situation is evidence of ability in a certain operation of memory. Excellence in foreign language demands a certain operation of memory. The high correlation between the recall of a particular situation and Foreign Languages indicates that the two operations of memory referred to are either the same or have some common factor.

(2) No explanation for the small correlations found in (2), (3), (4) and (5) is attempted, further than to offer the theory that those able in science are rather slow but sure in their thot processes and therefore the tendency is to longer reaction times.

(6) Repetition of words is considered by Jung and Riklin# as evidence of a limited vocabulary. Excellence in foreign languages is closely connected with the possession of a large vocabulary. In explanation of the high correalation between Foreign Languages and the 2'd Articulatory class (Repetitions) the theory is advanced that the mental condition in which there is difficulty in learning a foreign vocabulary is the same as, or intimately connected with the mental condition in which the repetition of words in the association experiment occurs.

(7) Regarding the function of visual imagery: Some, at least, of the introspections exhibit visual imagery as a mediating factor in the association process, i.e. a necessary link between stimulus and reaction, e.g. observor A #15, stimulus "truth", reaction "u",

#Journal für Neurologie & Psychologie, 1903-04 - Diagnostische Assoziation Studien.

time of reaction 1.8 sec., introspection "Strong visual image of the word 'truth' spelled out. Search for a related word finally discontinued and reaction 'u' because of its vividness in the word 'truth'. There was no attempt to prevent vocalization of the letter, since I had no thot that it would not meet the condition of the experiment which requires that the reaction shall be a word." The introspection indicates that the visual imagery mediated between stimulus and reaction.# However, most of the visual imagery can be explained as attendant imagery, e.g. observor B #71, stimulus "habit", reaction "instinct", time of reaction 1.7 sec., introspection "Visual image of the Natural History Building, then of the Physiological laboratory, then of the Zoological laboratory at Chicago, then of an unbound copy of the Journal of Animal Psychology, then of an article, apparently by Yerkes, then Lloyd Morgan's book 'Habit and Instinct'." In by far the majority of cases of visual imagery the association is less elaborate than the case just cited. The following is an illustration of a large class; stimulus "beauty", reaction "girl", introspection "I had a visual image of a beautiful girl." In such an association the belief that the visual imagery is merely attendant is less involved than in the illustration given before, but there is little difference in principle between the two. If visual imagery is simply attendant to the process of association and is not in general a mediating factor then it is unecessary and possibly a disturbing influence and it may be that those without it spend that energy in more productive processes and therefore rank highest in scholastic work. This conclusion is in agreement with the finding of Galton that men of science are peculiarly lacking in visual imagery.

#For further illustrations see; observor A #19, 20, 39, 53, etc.; observor B #16, 54, 63, etc.; etc.

(8) An analysis of certain of the fundamental conceptions of mathematics and science may reveal a reason for the correlation of .37 between each of these subjects and the group Alpha, (Synonyms, Contrast and Coordination). Such a conception as that of the surd roots of a quadratic equation involves the idea of coordination and contrast very explicitly. All conceptions involving inverse operations, e.g. differentiation and integration. are definitely concepts of contrast. Mathematical operations, such as solutions of equations, definitely involve concepts of equality or identity, which is very similar to the conception involved in the giving of synonyms. Considering the similarity of process in mathematics and in the comparison and contrasting of equivalent names, it is not surprising that there is a correlation between Mathematics and group Alpha, but rather that the correlation is not larger than is indicated in the table.

The high correlation between Mathematics and Science is in itself sufficient to account for most of the correlation between Science and the group Alpha.

The correlation between the group Alpha and Foreign Languages, .19, is smaller than a consideration of the importance of synonyms in foreign language work would lead one to anticipate. A correlation coefficient, not shown in the table, between Foreign Languages and Synonyms gives the correlation as .34.

The classification contains no group comparable to Jung's Definition class. Such a reaction as the following; stimulus "father", reaction "the chief of the family" Jung cites# as belonging to the Definition class. His conclusions that the Definition type of reac-

#20th Anniversary Lectures of Clark University.

tion is a simulated type and is evidence of low mentality do not apply to the Synonym class in this experiment for the following reasons; (a) There would be few, if any, reactions found in the Synonym class in this experiment, which would precisely correspond to Jung's Definition class. (b) The postulate of simulation is a theory of explanation and not a fact of evidence. While simulation has been the subject of considerable investigation a definite criterion thereof is still lacking. There is no ground for the assumption that the reactions here classsified as Synonyms are simulated.

The results obtained in this experiment point to the fact that reactions with synonyms involve a high type of ability in scholastic pursuits.

(9) The Gamma group is composed as follows: 54 per cent Predicates and Judgments of Quality, 33 per cent Coexistence, and 13 per cent Subordination. Things can coexist in a very large number of ways and, as already explained, the reactions were put into this class only when they could not satisfactorily be put into another. It follows that the reactions in this class are heterogeneous and high correlation between Coexistence and scholastic work could not be expected. The mental processes involved in naming predicates of an object are quite similar to those concerned in Subordination. The naming of predicates is neither a particularly difficult, nor a particularly simply task, but is quite colorless and on a more or less automatic level. Because of the nature of the three classes composing the group Gamma, one could anticipate only slight correlation of this group with scholastic attainments. The small correlations that the data yields are in this order - positive for Science (where the importance of the naming of predicates is probably the most pronounc-

ed), positive, but smaller, for Foreign Languages, negative for Mathematics.

(10) The group Beta (Subject Relation, Object Relation, Causality) has only 8 percent of the total number of observations in it and is not considered as reliable as the Alpha group, with 31 per cent, or the Gamma group with 36 per cent. The description of the observations put into this group shows that in the mind of the classifier there is a close connection between this group and the class Phrase Completion. In other words it seems that the naming of an abject when a verb is given, e.g. "hit" - "horse", and the naming of a subject when the verb is given, e.g. "eat" - "boy", is an association involving as little abstract thinking as a Phrase Completion association, when compared with the thot processes involved in a logical association such as Coordination, Contrast, or Synonyms. The correlation between group Beta and Phrase Completion is .15, with a probable error of .19 and if the data were more extensive a decided correlation might be found. No great weight is placed upon the correlation found with this group because of the known paucity of data, but nevertheless it is believed that such high negative correlations as it shows are significant of the general undesirability of the Beta group type of reaction.

(11) On account of the lack of definite knowledge as to the significance of variability in whatever test it may occur, the correlations found in (11), (12) and (13) are not interpreted. Their correct interpretation would undoubtedly involve a basic study into the nature of variability.

The entire trend of this investigation points to the fact that (1) the free association experiment yields results which are indica-

tive of the ability of the observors; (2) that the most significant features that are favorably correlated with scholastic rank in Mathematics, Science and Foreign Languages are (a) capability in the recall of a Particular Situation (b) frequency of reaction with Synonyms, Coordination and Contrast; (3) that the most significant features that are unfavorably correlated are (a) frequency of visual imagery (b) frequency of repetitions (c) frequency of reactions with Subject Relation, Object Relation and Causality; (4) that the data, as well as a consideration of the groups, suggests that the Alpha group (Synonyms, Contrast and Coordination) method of reaction involves greater ability than the Gamma group (Predicates, Subordination and Coexistence), which is in turn superior to the Beta group (Subject Relation, Object Relation and Causality) method.

F I N I S

APPENDIX.

Observor - A.

No.	Stimulus	Time	Reaction	Introspection
1	arch	1.8	wood	Temporary loss of association and then "wood" said just to say something.
2	prude	2.2	mean	Visual image of prudish girl I once knew. General feeling that prudishness was a "mean" state.
3	egotism	2.0	me	A short time spent in getting the word in mind, the "go" standing out prominently visually. Central tendency of egotism led to "me".
4	single	1.2	man	Vocal motor reaction. "Single man" a well known expression.
5	chastity	.6	good	Visual image of a girl. Then connection of the idea "good" with chastity.
6	ginger	1.4	pepper	Association untraceable.
7	shrew	1.0	bad	Visual image of an old hag and thot of the Pilgrims and of burning witches, in visual imagery. "Bad" was connected with this last.
8	adapt	1.0	quick	"apt" stood visually. Connection with "quick" obscure, but reaction seemed satisfactory at the time.
9	tough	1.2	boy	Visual image of a big tough boy.
10	morality	1.4	pure	Tendency to say "good" inhibited. Slight visual image of word "pure". Purity thot of as being a parallel quality with morality.
11	rubber	1.0	look	Familiarity with the expression "rubber neck" gave rise to image of person looking. Visual imagery.
12	coquet	1.0	good	Former reaction (See 5&7) affected this one. First was an impulse to say "bad" and then its opposite.
13	kick	1.4	horse	Visual image of a boy kicking, then search for more appropriate symbol and saw a horse kicking.
14	forward	1.4	backward	Visual image of a deep forest brought up because "forest" and "forward" are somewhat similar. Reason for choice of the word "backward" difficult to ascertain.
15	truth	1.8	you (or) u	The reaction was really "u". Strong visual image of the word spelled out. Search for a related word finally given up and reacted to "u" because of its vividness.
16	cake	1.4	good	Visual memory image of eating cake in the pantry.
17	skeptic	1.0	good	The word "good" came into my mind together with the idea that it was a senseless association, but it was said before it could be inhibited.

Observor - A.

No.	Stimulus	Time	Reaction	Introspection
18	extort	1.8	yell	Visual image of "ort" and of a ranting politician. Saw him yelling at the crowd.
19	modest	1.4	boy	Visual image of a modest boy. I wished to say "girl" but to be true to the image said "boy".
20	religion	1.0	I	Strong visual image of "gion". Influenced by a preceding reaction(15) I reacted to the letter "i". The letter "i" stood out clearly in a bright, slightly violet light.
21	knife	1.0	cut	Visual image of a butcher knife ready to cut.
22	fanatic	2.2	wild	Visual image of a woman with staring eyes. Search for word meaning the same. "Wild" was inadequate.
23	insult	1.4	me	Probable connection with previous reaction (3). None or little visual imagery. "Insult" seemed to have a central tendency.
24	flaxen	1.6	curls	Visual image of auburn haired little girl with flaxen curls.
25	soul	1.4	hazy	Visual image of a transparent man. This may have been called up by a reaction in a different experiment. The outline of the man was hazy.
26	bar	2.0	growl	Doubt as to the stimulus caused delay in reacting. I thot it was "bark" and I had a visual image of a dog.
27	president	2.0	big	Visual image of President Taft, with certain of his personal traits well indicated.
28	fluster	2.0	fly	Saw the word spelled out and next the word "cluster", then a number of birds flying. Visual association between "fluster" and "cluster".
29	juicy	1.2	apple	Visual image of a bottle of juicy peaches, but the reaction was vocal motor using the expression "juicy apple".
30	death	1.8	bad	Visual image of the word. Search for an equivalent word in meaning. Then the realization that the word was unique and reacted with "bad" as being a quality of death. While reacting thot of "bad" as not necessarily being such a quality, i.e. death may not be bad.
31	press	2.2	squeeze	Decided muscular effort, including movement of the hands together. The movement was both to represent the word and an effort to pull out the word "squeeze" which came with difficulty.

Observor - A.

No.	Stimulus	Time	Reaction	Introspection
32	beauty	1.2	pretty	Visual image of American beauty rose. "Pretty" was not the word wanted because not "beautiful" enough.
33	retard	.8	slow	"Slow" seemed waiting for utterance. While responding had a visual image of "retard".
34	ghostly	1.1	bad	Visual image of white ghost and thot that many persons think ghosts are evil.
35	future	3.6	run	Stimulus given without forewarning and I was about to ask the experimentor to give it over when I thot that I could not do so because I knew the stimulus word, so I set myself to the task of reacting. All this without visual imagery. Now visual imagery came in and "run" was suggested because it has a "u" in it similar to the "u" in "ure". Only the last syllable of "future" was seen. Visual image of "run".
36	text	1.2	book	Feeling for association and then the simple vocal motor association "text-book".
37	success	1.6	brilliant	Visual image of rather bright light, white with a reddish tinge. "Brilliant"a very satisfactory reaction.
38	abstract	2.0	concrete	Search for some quality of "abstract" caused delay. "Abstract-concrete"remembered from a previous experiment.
39	fatalism	1.0	a	Strong visual image of an "a" in a red field. Meaning of the term came after I had reacted.
40	gauze	1.3	filmy	Visual image of a "filmy" lace skirt.
41	error	1.3	bad	Visual image of the word spelled out. Search for a word that was a synonym. Recognized errors as bad. Probably verbal.
42	gargle	1.2	giggle	Visual and kinesthetic image of gargling. Reaction undoubtedly articulatory.
43	energetic	1.0	fast	Visual image of the word - also of boy running down the street.
44	apathy	1.0	good	Visual image of a large dinner table with lots of people. Things looked "good". No organic imagery, but possible slight gustatory. (Stimulus mistaken for "apetite".)
45	silk	1.1	worm	Vocal motor.
46	stage	1.4	wood	Visual image of stage with scenery, caste, etc., and rag carpet on a splintered wood floor .
47	curse	1.2	he	"Me" was inhibited and "he" replaced it. Vocal motor.

Observor - A.

No.	Stimulus	Time	Reaction	Introspection
48	duty	1.4	you	Visual image of the word. I recalled the reaction for "truth" (15). The reaction this time was very similar.
49	valor	1.0	brave	Visual image of the word, especially "val". "Brave" suggested because it contained an "av" and because its meaning fitted well.
50	velvet	1.2	plush	Visual and cutaneous image of velvet. Then visual image of purple plush.
51	secure	1.2	safe	Meaning was clear and "safe" was given as a synonym. While reacting had a visual image of an iron safe.
52	giggle	1.6	gargle	Vocal motor reaction, probably induced by the reaction for "gargle"(42).
53	inhuman	1.0	man	Visual image of the word. The "man" on the end of the word led to the reaction. Meaning of the word fairly clear but no attempt to use the meaning in determining the reaction.
54	ecstacy	1.6	fast	Slight visual imagery of a person. Search for a word meaning some one who was thrilling with ecstacy. "Fast" rushed in, possibly because of the intensity of the emotion of the person visualized.
55	lace	1.2	curtain	Visual image of a lace curtain. Partly articulatory. Visual image of "lace".
56	hint	2.0	tell	Visual image of the word spelled out, especially of the "nt". Ineffectual search for synonym. Thot of expression "don't tell". Verbal imagery.
57	blush	1.4	red	Visual image of a pretty girl with red cheeks. The whole situation was very clearly imaged.
58	wicked	1.0	I	Visual image of the word and the "i" insisted upon coming out. I tried to inhibit it but too late.
59	conscience	1.2	me	Articulatory. The idea was that it was my conscience that was under consideration.
60	shoulder	1.3	strong	Visual image of brawny shoulders.
61	graft	1.2	bad	Visual image of a fat politician, of course a grafter, probably Lorimer.
62	behave	1.8	hard	Search for a word that was a synonym. I did not find it and "hard" came up. The word had occurred to me some minutes before for some reason or other.
63	sacrifice	2.0	beast	Visual image of the word, but associations arising from this inhibited. Visual image of a priest with a white coat. Then visual image of

Observor - A.

No.	Stimulus	Time	Reaction	Introspection
63				sacrificial pier with smoke rising. Wood was burning on the pier but I knew that a sacrifice should be of an animal. The visual image of the word containing a red "a" suggested the blood of an animal. The delay was caused by search for some such word as "goat" , "calf",etc.
64	philosophy	1.8	Daniels	Faint visual imagery of the word "philosophy", of Professor Daniels, and of the word "Daniels". (I am taking a course in philosophy under Professor Daniels).
65	trifle	1.3	little	Search for association, then the word "little". Channel of association obscure.
66	bedlam	1.2	mix up	Hazy visual image of Tower of Babel situation.
67	consent	1.8	let	Visual image of the word, also of a girl and her mother. The girl was pleading with her mother to "let her go out".
68	courage	---	---	(No reaction. The push given the stop watch set the hands back to the starting point and, of course, did not start the watch) The tick of the stop watch has been apparent during these tests, but in this case it did not work and I seemed to be unable to form associations without the sound of the watch. The fact of this dependence was quite startling, as I had not imagined it to exist.
68	courage	1.6	fast	(Performed later) Visual image of a boy running toward the foe, It was probably a snow ball fight.
69	cowardice	1.6	bad	Same visual image as for "courage" and in addition the image of a boy running away from the first one. No word came readily describing this and then "bad" jumped out.
70	course	2.0	big	Hunt for synonym - finally saw coarse sand composed of "big" grains.
71	habit	2.0	action	Visual image of the word, especially the letter "a", which was slightly red in color. Thot of expression "habit basis for action". Articulatory
72	gamble	2.0	wicked	Uncertainty as to the stimulus, finally deciding that it was "gamble". Visual image of a bleary-eyed man gambling.
73	purity	.8	woman	Visual image of a woman. Also faint visual image of the word "purity".

Observor - A.

No.	Stimulus	Time	Reaction	Introspection
74	drug	1.3	bad	Tendency to say "big" inhibited and "bad" said instead. The phrase "bad drug" may have been present.
75	snake	1.1	bite	Visual image of snake, but verbal reaction.
76	intention	1.6	good	Visual image of word and of phrase "good intention", partly visual and partly verbal.
77	caution	1.2	careful	Visual image of the word - of the "au" especially, which was dark in color. "Careful" represented the complex well.
78	alimony	2.0	good	Hesitancy in getting its meaning clear and then remembrance of a person who got alimony, which was most fortunate in that case.
79	atheism	2.4	evil	Visual image of a black fanatic in some southern country, probably India. Why he should stand for "atheism" is more than I can say. He certainly looked "evil" enough.
80	cuckoo	1.4	big	Hunt for association, but finding none responded with the easiest word. (See 74 and 70)
81	height	1.4	tall	Visual image of a tall building with a spire, also of a tall man whom I had just previously met.
82	deject	1.4	hurt	Visual image of a man with the blues, his elbows on his knees, etc., and the idea was that that condition was hurtful to him.
83	concept	2.0	suggestion	Visual image of a cloud of haze, representing the mental state before the concept is clearly built up. Search for a word with a hard "g" in it. This led to the word "suggestion". (Two days later the observer said that he knew that the word that was searched for was "vague". He did not know immediately after the reaction)
84	temperance	2.0	wine	Visual image of a saloon with lots of people. I tried to get a word picturing this whole situation but did not find it. Saw wine being poured out of a bottle.
85	chide	1.4	child	Visual image of the word. Search for a synonym which did not come so I reacted with "child" which I saw.
86	law	1.0	abiding	Visual image of the word "abiding". I think this followed a verbal image of the same word and that the reaction was started from the verbal image.

Observor - A.

No.	Stimulus	Time	Reaction	Introspection
87	virtue	1.6	woman	Visual image of a woman. Very similar to the image for "purity". (73)
88	reverse	1.2	turn	Visual image of a wheel, particularly the upper part of it. Felt satisfaction in noting that "reverse" was well represented by the fact that the circular wheel was reversible.
89	handsome	1.4	pretty	Visual image of a handsome man with red cheeks. "Pretty" poorly expressed the situation, but was an easy reaction.
90	temper	2.2	mean	Visual image of a bad little boy and almost responded with "bad", but inhibited it and responded with a similar meaning word.
91	heaven	1.2	ly	Visual image of "heaven" in a bright light. Reaction, however, was verbal, being the last part of "heavenly". I did not realize at the time of reaction that "ly" was not a word.
92	quitter	1.6	stop	Thot of the meaning of the term. No visual imagery.
93	thrill	1.2	shake	Visual image of the word, especially the "r" and of a person trembling with ecstacy. "Shake" was a very poor representative of the complex.
94	character	.8	sketch	Entirely verbal. While reacting I had a visual image of "sketch" in a bright light.
95	thief	1.2	rob	Thot of meaning. Also visual image of thief at the pantry window. This image was a common one in childhood, tho not a memory of any actual experience.
96	guile	1.2	bad	Temporary inability to get the meaning of the term. The word "bad" rushed out. Verbal.
97	bully	1.2	good	Thot of Roosevelt. "Good" came without effort and with little connection with "Roosevelt". Verbal.
98	revel	2.2	wicked	Thot of Mexican rebels (stimulus mistaken for "rebel") and felt for word "insurrectos", which did not come.
99	revenge	2.0	soak	Visual image of a percon hitting another and thot "soak 'im one".
100	iniquity	1.8	hurt	Immediate tendency to say "bad". Visual image of the word, especially the "qui" and the feeling that iniquity was hurtful.

Observor - B.

No.	Stimulus	Time	Reaction	Introspection
1	arch	1.2	round	Visual image of an arch with a peak. "Round" came from the fact that arches in general have a bend.
2	prude	1.2	woman	My experiments came back to me and I recognized it as a word out of my own list. I tried to think of something of a slang nature that was derogatory, such as "silly person". Later I got a faint visual image of a girl, which led to the response "woman".
3	egotism	1.3	person	Vivid visual image of an egotistical friend of mine. His name did not come and just why "person" was said is not clear.
4	single	.8	person	"Single-man" recalled as a very frequent reaction in my experiments. Probably in the preceding reaction as in this, there was a tendency to say "man", but "person" forced its way out. "Person" came with a rush, probably due to the preceding reaction.
5	chastity	2.5	girl	Disturbed by possible ambiguity of the word, thinking that the word might have ended in "ive". When I discovered that the word was "chastity" I applied it to the female sex having a vague visual image of a number of women or girls.
6	ginger	1.2	sharp	Another word came in first just as "sharp" was being formed. This word was "bite". Visual image of can of ginger with spoon and of mouth opening and apparent presence of ginger on the tongue. Slight cutaneous sensation of ginger.
7	shrew	1.3	woman	Wonder whether the stimulus was "shrew" or "shrewd". No visual imagery. Thot that if the word was "shrew" the reaction was sensible.
8	adapt	3.0	fit	Thot the word was something like "agagt". After deciding the word was "adapt" I recalled that it was a word in my own experiment and that Mr ___ had reacted with "fit". Remembered puzzling whether "fit" had been used by Mr ___ as a synonym for adapt. This was in connection with the adaptation of species in order to "fit" in with their environment. Imagery was kinesthetic - a very little visual imagery of "agagt".
9	tough	1.3	nut	Took the word to mean "morally tough". I thot of the general tough lad of

Observor - B.

No.	Stimulus	Time	Reaction	Introspection
9				18 or 20. Response kinesthetic.
10	morality	1.1	woman	Repetition of preceding reaction for "chastity". In this case there was no visual imagery.
11	rubber	1.9	flexible	Visual image of rubber band and kinesthetic sensation of pulling it. Desire for the word "elastic" but it did not come. Just as "flexible" was being said thot of solid rubber which could be bent.
12	coquet	.9	girl	Visual image of a girl in a coquetish attitude, especially as to the eyes, etc. This is likely a picture originally created by reading one of the Heisenflipper articles in the Illini.
13	kick	.6	hard	Visual image of someone, possibly myself, kicking something on the ground. Slight leg strain.
14	forward	1.1	person	Visual image of an excessively energetic "forward" youth. Articulatory conflict between "person" and some other word which contained a hard "g". I did not remember until after the response that "person" was a reaction that I had made before.
15	truth	1.1	honesty	Visual image of a person. Recognized "truth" as a quality of an ideal person and searched for another quality. This was largely in articulatory terms.
16	cake	1.7	sweet	Visual image of frosty cake. Desired to say something like "delicious". Entirely visual. Sweet suggested by the frosting. No gustatory experience.
17	skeptic	1.0	man	I am not sure whether or not this reaction was given in my tests. Visual image just as I was speaking of an old man, possibly a preacher, etc. "Man" came as a placement or example of skeptic. Articulatory.
18	extort	.7	money	Faint visual image of Spanish inquisition, rack, etc. Just before saying "money" one of the black rogues resolved himself into a Mr ___ who is a Jew and who gave this reaction in my experiment. The history of the case in my mind was in the reverse order, e. i. the visual imagery etc. came from a study of Mr ___'s reaction.
19	modest	1.0	girl	Visual image of a girl, etc. sitting in a room. She had a rather bashful appearance. No traceable connection

Observor - B.

No.	Stimulus	Time	Reaction	Introspection.
20	religion	1.0	God	Tendency to name some religious sect or church body. The name for this did not come and then the notion of God as a part of the whole religious complex. Articulatory. Vague visual imagery of people.
21	knife	.8	cut	Visual image of knife, blade pointing over left shoulder. The word "sharp" came in, probably a perseveration of the reaction before for "ginger".
22	fanatic	1.1	man	Vivid visual image of some such character as Peter the Hermit - a man with a very black beard with a little brown and grey in it, with wild eyes, etc. Slight tendency to say "woman". "Woman" was a reaction occurring in my own experiment.
23	insult	1.0	harm	This came out of my own experiment, meaning of neither word particularly thot of. Articulatory.
24	flaxen	.9	hair	I had to think twice to catch the word. Visual image of child, etc. with flaxen hair.
25	soul	1.2	hope	Visual image of a man, a semi-transparent person, the trunk and head only standing out clearly. Within his breast was a white cloud, representing his soul. Tendency to say something indicating this person when the word "hope" came with a rush. This reaction was in my own experiment.
26	bar	2.2	keeper	Very conscious of delay on account of misunderstanding whether "bar" or "bark". Then, not recalling the "k" sound, repeated with "keeper". Thot of "bark" as dog's bark and the bark of a tree. Later a visual image of a sand bar and also the bar of a saloon.
27	president	1.4	Harper	Thot first of presidents of the United States-Roosevelt, Abraham Lincoln, McKinley, Taft, in quick succession and searched for the name of one of these people. All of a sudden "Harper" came out. This was a reaction in my own experiment.
28	fluster	1.0	man	Visual image of a young man surrounded by a crowd that was asking questions and the man was very much embarrassed. "Flustered" represented the situation. The man was the center of it. The signs of the

Observor - B.

No.	Stimulus	Time	Reaction	Introspection
28				man's embarrassment were visual, in his attitude, etc.
29	juicy	.7	apple	Visual image of apple, etc.
30	death	.9	life	Visual image of a funeral ceremony, etc. Reaction was articularly, representing a contrast such as the preacher might be pointing out. The idea of contrast developed after reacting.
31	press	1.0	hard	Visual image of a tailor shop with a negro pressing trousers. First tendency was to react with "clothes". The effort the negro was making suggested "hard".
32	beauty	1.3	woman	Visual image of a certain woman singer and then of a very beautiful woman.
33	retard	.8	slow	Purely articulatory reaction out of my own experiment.
34	ghostly	.8	spirit	Visual image of a person in a white sheet, succeeded by that of a transparent person, etc. (See 25)
35	future	.5	hope	Vague visual image of a young man. Articulatory reaction out of my own experiment.
36	text	.6	book	Recalled previous experiment and the reaction "Angel - book". "Angel" came first and "book" second. Responded with "book" because it was easier. Articulatory.
37	success	1.0	happy	Same visual image as for "future" (35), except more distinct, particularly the man's face which was smiling and "happy."
38	abstract	1.0	concrete	First meaning I got was to "take away from". The contrast leading to the reaction was articulatory.
39	fatalism	3.4	Indian	There was first a repetition of the word and a dwelling on it to get the full significance of it. Then a visual image of a map of the lower part of Asia. No word came. Finally images of Indians, etc. Map of Asia came back again, particularly of India and I started to react with "India" and while doing so added the "n".
40	gauze	1.2	white	Visual image of cheese cloth and had my mouth fixed to say "thin" when the word "white" displaced it as being more appropriate to cheese cloth.
41	error	1.1	way	Articulatory. I thot of the phrase "point out the error of his way".
42	gargle	1.0	throat	Visual-verbal image of the word "gargoyl". In my experiments the word

Observor - B.

No.	Stimulus	Time	Reaction	Introspection
42				"gargle" was mistaken for "gorgoyl." Visual image of a person gargling.
43	energetic	1.0	man	Same visual imagery that I had in regard to "success". (37)
44	apathy	.8	man	Same as preceding. Alongside of this fellow was another man, just the opposite.
45	silk	1.0	thin	Visual image of a greenish-blue skirt. The thinness was not so apparent as the wavyness of it. "Thin" probably came because it had just been repeated. (See 40)
46	stage	.8	coach	Similar reaction in my experiment. Decided visual image of a stage-coach, etc.
47	curse	.8	hard	In the sense of a "hard" character. This is a reaction out of my experiment. Faint visual image of a tough looking specimen. Reaction largely articulatory.
48	duty	.9	man	Rather faint visual image of a face, or rather a succession of faces, in rapid order. Kinesthetic sensation that accompanies the feeling of straining to do one's duty.
49	valor	.9	man	Visual image of a number of cadets, with guns, and showing an all too conscious bravery.
50	velvet	1.2	smooth	Visual image of black velvet. The kinesthetic-cutaneous quality of it is what appealed to me more than the smoothness of it. Smooth was the only word that came.
51	secure	.5	man	Visual image of Tantulus secured to the rocks.
52	giggle	1.3	girl	Started to say "laugh" when "girl" swept it away. Visual image of a girl giggling. The first tendency to say "laugh" was probably articulatory.
53	inhuman	.7	man	Visual image of a man behaving brutally toward someone else.
54	ecstacy	1.0	girl	Do not know whether religious ecstacy or some other kind. Visual image of a girl in a rapt state of emotion.
55	lace	1.0	curtain	Visual image of curtain, etc.
56	hint	3.0	word	Inhibited the word "man". Visual image of a man with a certain expression on his face of looking out of the corner of his eyes. "Word" came slowly, connected with the idea of the "hint" being conveyed by "word".

Observor - B.

No.	Stimulus	Time	Reaction	Introspection
57	blush	1.0	person	Visual image of red-cheeked young girl.
58	wicked	.8	girl	Same visual image. Wicked taken rather in the sense of being the cause of the blush.
59	conscience	1.0	man	Same visual image as I got for ghostly, i.e. of a transparent man with a little white cloud in his breast, which was his conscience.
60	shoulder	2.2	man	First idea was strong. Visual image of a strong,powerful shoulder. Entirely visual. The mental reaction was to the strength of it. Then visual image of a woman's shoulder and nearly reacted 'woman' the word 'man' replaced it.
61	graft	2.0	politician	Visual image of the corner in Danville where the car turns. Also image of a fat sleek'politician'near the hotel, but the word came with difficulty.
62	behave	1.0	girl	Probably due to having reacted with 'girl' before. Visual image of a young girl who apparently was behaving perfectly well.
63	sacrifice	2.0	alter	Visual image of old Jewish alters and burnt offerings and I wanted to say the name of some animal but could not get it out. Finally the alter itself led to the reaction.
64	philosophy	1.0	Daniels	Visual image of Professor Daniels' office. Professor Daniels stood for philosophy to me.
65	trifle	2.0	affections	The word "feelings" competed very strongly with "affections", all three words containing "f". Remembrance of my own experiment. I was conscious of the different meaning of the word "trifle". The definite remembrance that this reaction was one occurring in my own experiment came after my reaction.
66	bedlam	1.3	insane asylum	Articularly reaction coming from my own experiment. No visual imagery.
67	consent	1.3	girl	Visual image of a girl, but the idea impressed was not particularly connected with this picture. The idea was "consent to marry".
68	courage	3.0	hope	The word "man" came immediately. No visual imagery. In the avoidance of the word "man" I seemed to be at a mental standstill. Next came a grouping for other qualities, like "courage", which finally came as

Observor - B.

No.	Stimulus	Time	Reaction	Introspection
68				"faith, hope, charity".
69	cowardice	1.2	girl	Visual image of a girl standing near a corner, with other girls in the vicinity. The girl was shrinking back from crossing the street.
70	course	.8	philosophy	I thot of courses in the university. The word "philosophy" probably was due to previous reaction for "philosophy". While reacting I was aware of the ambiguity of the term.
71	habit	1.7	instinct	Visual image of the Natural History building, then of the physiological laboratory, then of the zoological laboratory at Chicago, then of the Journal of Animal Psychology, an unbound copy of it, then of an article, apparently by Yerkes, then Lloyd Morgan's book "Habit and Instinct".
72	gamble	1.0	man	Visual image of an entire room full of gambling devices, with men playing, etc. In the foreground of the picture was a very young man, etc.
73	purity	1.0	girl	Visual image of a girl, apparently in a doctor's office. There was nothing in the imagery to convey the idea, which was that of sexual purity. Probably the frequent reaction "girl" influenced this one.
74	drug	.8	store	Visual image of a drug store.
75	snake	.9	grass	Visual image of a little green grass snake in the grass. "Grass" came from the latter.
76	intention	2.0	girl	Tried to inhibit "girl" but could not do it. Extremely faint visual imagery. The general situation seemed to take place near the library. The girl might have been jollying some chap. "Girl" came immediately to my mind.
77	caution	1.7	girl	This came out of my own experiment. The feeling is that someone is cautioning a girl against indiscrete behavior. Slight visual imagery - mainly articulatory.
78	alimony	1.0	divorce	Articulatory. Very little meaning in either of these words. They are simply attached together as words.
79	atheism	.9	God	Recognized after I said the word "God" that there was more contrast between the words than I had anticipated at the time of reaction. Reaction was articulatory. The words are connected without much meaning.

Observor - B.

No.	Stimulus	Time	Reaction	Introspection
80	cuckoo	.9	clock	Word completion reaction. After speaking "clock" I had a visual image of a clock, etc. I make the following distinction between articulatory and word completion reactions; in an articulatory reaction there is a strain in the throat, while in a word completion reaction there is no such strain and the word flows without effort.
81	height	.9	weight	Articulatory. No visual imagery until after I had reacted. Stimulus and reaction were considered as attributes of some body unrepresented.
82	deject	1.0	person	Visual image of the room in the laboratory at Chicago, etc. Then a visual image of an old man whom I have seen and who has a dejected bearing. Recalled my own experiment and the difficulty of reacting to deject. The reaction was articulatory, out of my own experiment.
83	concept	1.3	logic	Slow in catching the word. Visual image of Bode. Feeling for Bode's name and would have reacted with it if it had come. "Logic" was connected with this visual image.
84	temperance	1.3	movement	Visual image of scene in Chicago in front of Willard building. The word I was most receptive to was something like "extension". Failing this "movement" came. Fleeting visual image of crowds being addressed, etc. No word completion idea.
85	chide	1.0	hard	"Hard" was not the word I wanted. I thot of a child being scolded very energetically. The energy used was the reason for reacting with "hard". "Vigorously" would have been a better word.
86	law	1.0	school	A little hesitation as to the word. Visual image of the law building and one of the men there. No word completion idea. As to the hesitation preceding apperception of the stimulus, which is present in practically all the reactions, it is about like this: The stimulus word as first heard always differs more or less from the word as apperceived. Some sounds are either added to it or taken away, the inflection may be changed, etc. be-

Observor - B.

No.	Stimulus	Time	Reaction	Introspection
86				fore it gets into the form that is reacted to; i. e. I react to a construct of my own and not to something that is simply given.
87	virtue	1.0	vice	Articulatory. However I had a fleeting visual image of a girl probably connected with the idea of virtue. I have spoken this combination of words "virtue - vice" within the last half hour, in speaking to Mr ___.
88	reverse	2.1	chair	The tendency at the first was to give "obverse", but it did not come. There was a blocking on this account. There was throat strain occasioned by the repetition of the word "reverse", especially the last syllable. I had my eyes open and noticed the chair and while staring at it there came into my mind the idea of a reversible chair. It was a case where the word stimulus was woven into the present experience.
89	handsome	.8	woman	Visual image of a handsome woman.
90	temper	1.6	child	Strain sensation trying to say several words - "man", "woman", "people", "person". As soon as I was conscious of this block I gave it up and immediately got a visual image of a little child.
91	heaven	.8	hell	Fleeting visual image of the pearly gates, etc. Reaction, however, was articulatory.
92	quitter	1.0	coward	Articulatory. Recognized "quitter" as being one of my words and the reaction as one occurring in my experiment. Faint visual imagery of the word "quitter".
93	thrill	1.1	patriotism	Visual image of a girl looking up into the sky. In this connection I would probably have reacted "thrill of emotion". This did not come and "patriotism" rolled in in articulatory fashion out of the group of complexes of my own experiment.
94	character	1.9	virtue	Faint visual image of the back of a theater, etc., with one of the characters on the stage. Then the stimulus was thot of as an attribute of a person and there was a search for another attribute. Articulatory.

Observor - B.

No.	Stimulus	Time	Reaction	Introspection
95	thief	.6	robber	Visual image of a robber, etc. The reaction was of the word-completion type - I thot of the phrase "a thief and a robber".
96	guile	5.0	I	"I give up". I knew perfectly well that the stimulus was not "Guild" but the visual image of Mr Guild came so strongly that it blocked everything else. It was the consciousness of being wrong that created the block. My efforts to get away from this block took this direction: "English department," "rhetoric", etc. Since the original stimulus still did not fit I failed to respond.
97	bully	1.0	fellow	There was a little feeling of strain trying to get something to attach the word to. I might have said "bully time", "bully crowd", etc. As I was reacting I had several visual images - the last of a nicely dressed young chap.
98	revel	1.3	night	Visual image of a banquet table surrounded with knights and ladies. The reaction was an articulatory completion of "revelry by night".
99	revenge	1.0	tragedy	Thot of a tragedy as being the affect of revenge. There was first a preparation to see something like a killing, but there was no visual imagery. This reaction occurred in my experiments. Reaction mainly articulatory - some kinesthetic imagery.
100	iniquity	.9	sin	Visual image of "iniquity". Thot of it as an attribute of mankind and sin thot of as a synonym. Articulatory.

Observor - C.

No.	Stimulus	Time	Reaction	Introspection
1	arch	2.0	foot	Verbal. I thot of the arch of my foot. I have had trouble with the arches of my feet, tho I did not think of that fact at the time of reaction.
2	prude	1.6	old maid	Visual image of a tall and slender, disdainful looking person.
3	egotism	4.4	conceit	No visual image. Search for a word finally came to a verbal definition of it. First there was a feeling of suspension and sort of diffuse groping. Not conscious of any muscular strain or anything similar to it.
4	single	1.4	one	Verbal, no visual imagery.
5	chastity	1.1	purity	Verbal definition.
6	ginger	1.3	hot	Cutaneous image of slight burning on the tip of my tongue. No taste of ginger.
7	shrew	1.8	taming of the shrew	Verbal.
8	adapt	2.8	get used to	Verbal.
9	tough	1.4	beef	Purely verbal. Memory of a piece of steak I had recently.
10	morality	8.0	---	(No reaction.) Search for anything that would go with morality, but seemed to know of nothing that went with it. After the indicated time I thot of "morality plays".
11	rubber	1.1	show	Verbal.
12	coquet	4.4	Miss ---	Distinct visual image of Miss ---, with a smile, etc. Inhibited reaction because I did not wish to say her name. (Time would have been about 1.4)
13	kick	2.0	football	Visual image of a football lying on the ground.
14	forward	1.1	go	Verbal.
15	truth	2.3	right	Verbal definition.
16	cake	1.4	sweet	Gustatory image, rather indistinct. No visual imagery.
17	skeptic	2.5	philosopher	Verbal. Thot of that class of philosophers - the Skeptics.
18	extort	1.7	get	Verbal. The word I responded with a definition, but the reaction was so easy that there was no search or particular effort.
19	modest	1.4	shy	Verbal definition.

Observor - C.

No.	Stimulus	Time	Reaction	Introspection
20	religion	4.0	Presbyterian	First there was a confused and entirely indefinite search for something to fit with "religion". Verbal.
21	knife	1.0	sharp	Visual image of the bright blade of a pen-knife, etc.
22	fanatic	.9	crazy	Verbal.
23	insult	1.6	mad	Verbal. The idea of insult and the affect it usually has.
24	flaxen	1.0	yellow	Thot of yellow hair,in verbal terms. No visual imagery.
25	soul	5.0	I	No imagery. Mental groping. ("I can't associate a thing ..." was finally said and the time taken, tho it was not meant as a reaction).
26	bar	1.7	crow bar	Verbal.
27	president	1.1	Roosevelt	Verbal.
28	fluster	5.0	---	(No reaction) The meaning of the word was clear, but no association. Impatience at not getting an association, with movement of the hands as a sort of relief from the nervous tension.
28	fluster	2.1	bother	Verbal. The first feeling was amusement at memory of the previous failure. (Performed later)
29	juicy	1.1	orange	Cutaneous, or possibly gustatory image. Sense of orange juice in the mouth.
30	death	4.8	sadness	Absolute bewilderment at first. Finally a purely verbal reaction. No concrete instance in mind, tho recently one has been in my experience.
31	press	1.0	paper	Verbal. The "press" stands for the "daily paper".
32	beauty	1.2	rose	Verbal. Why I said "rose" instead of "American beauty" is not clear.
33	retard	1.6	slack	Verbal.
34	ghostly	1.7	white	Flitting visual image, bright and luminous.
35	future	5.6	I	No concrete imagery. A feeling of indefinite time, if such a thing is possible. ("I can't get a reaction for that, either" was finally said and the time taken, tho it was not meant as a reaction.)
36	text	.9	book	Verbal.
37	success	1.3	prosperity	Verbal.
38	abstract	3.8	take away	Feeling for some word that fitted. "Take away" was the first thing that came

Observor - C.

No.	Stimulus	Time	Reaction	Introspection
38				It did not exactly suit the feeling.
39	fatalism	9.0	your	(No reaction) "Your words are too much for me". My first impulse was to get some definite concrete association. The meaning was perfectly clear. I had the idea that I could discuss it at length, but no single word came. Entirely verbal.
40	gauze	.9	thin	Verbal.
41	error	.7	mistake	Verbal definition. Reaction seemed to be a matter of habit.
42	gargle	2.6	throat	Kinesthetic imagery of the action of gargling.
43	energetic	1.2	busy	Verbal.
44	apathy	4.8	feelingness	Verbal reaction - a sort of a definition.
45	silk	1.0	soft	Verbal and partly tactual. The feeling of foulard silk as you run your hand over it.
46	stage	1.0	actress	Verbal.
47	curse	1.2	swear	Verbal.
48	duty	.8	bound	Completed the phrase "duty bond" and was aware of giving the entire phrase. This is the first time that I have been aware of repeating the stimulus
49	valor	1.1	courage	Verbal.
50	velvet	.8	soft	Verbal with possibly slight cutaneous sensation.
51	secure	.7	safe	Verbal.
52	giggle	.7	laugh	Verbal.
53	inhuman	1.4	unkind	Verbal.
54	ecstacy	1.1	joy	Verbal. These reactions seem to be automatic with no imagery.
55	lace	1.3	white	Visual image of a window full of laces that I was looking at yesterday.
56	hint	6.2	suggestion	There was an attitude and struggle, but nothing came up clearly.
57	blush	.9	red	Verbal.
58	wicked	.8	sinful	Verbal.
59	conscience	1.3	right	Verbal. There was a sort of a vague wondering what consciousness really is.

,Observor - C.

No.	Stimulus	Time	Reaction	Introspection
60	shoulder	.6	blade	Verbal. Completion of an idea.
61	graft	1.4	Chicago	Verbal. I immediately thot of the newspaper write-ups of Chicago grafting.
62	behave	.7	well	Phrase completion.
63	sacrifice	3.6	self	There was a blank at first, then the phrase "self sacrifice". Verbal.
64	philosophy	.6	of life	Phrase completion. The general notion of somebody's philosophy of life.
65	trifle	4.1	of little account	Verbal definition.
66	bedlam	.9	noise	Just as the stimulus was given there was a noise in the hall.
67	consent	1.7	assent	Verbal.
68	courage	1.1	bravery	Verbal definition.
69	cowardice	1.8	afraid	Verbal, accompanied by a feeling of amusement.
70	course	1.0	race	Inverted phrase completion. Thot of "race course".
71	habit	2.0	fixed	Verbal. I did not think of the phrase "fixed habit" - it was rather a definition.
72	gamble	1.2	money	Verbal. I did not think of any of the methods of gambling, but only of the money lost.
73	purity	2.0	chastity	Verbal.
74	drug	1.3	reel	Verbal. I did not think of any phrase and do not know why I should have gotten "reel". No visual imagery.
75	snake	1.7	delirium tremens	I would not have given this reaction if it had not followed the preceding. Purely verbal.
76	intention	1.0	good	Phrase completion idea, inverted.
77	caution	1.5	careful	Verbal.
78	alimony	1.0	divorce	Verbal. Reactions such as this one do not refer to any particular instance.
79	atheism	1.9	disbelief	Verbal. The word I wanted was "unbelief".
80	cuckoo	.9	clock	Phrase completion. After reacting I got a visual image of a clock.
81	height	1.0	tall	Verbal.
82	deject	1.3	forlorn	Phrase completion idea. "Dejected and forlorn".
83	concept	1.0	idea	Verbal. Afterward reacting there flashed thru my mind discussions on this topic.
84	temperance	3.2	abstinence	Verbal definition.

Observor - C.

No.	Stimulus	Time	Reaction	Introspection
85	chide	.8	scold	Verbal.
86	law	1.0	and order	Phrase completion.
87	virtue	2.8	good	Verbal. The interval was filled with a struggle and I think I frowned.
88	reverse	1.6	turn about	Verbal.
89	handsome	.9	good looking	Verbal.
90	temper	1.3	anger	Verbal.
91	heaven	2.2	sky	The first thot was a hazy memory of the stories I used to hear about heaven. It was always spoken of as being in the sky.
92	quitter	7.0	horse	(Mistook the stimulus for "critter") A hazy notion of a down eastern farmer talking about a critter. This must have come from something that I have read. I connected the name "Silas" with it. No visual imagery. I felt that I had to give some word reaction and gave "horse."
93	thrill	1.8	ecstacy	Verbal. I think the previous reaction to ecstacy (54) influenced this one.
94	character	1.1	good	Verbal.
95	thief	1.0	steal	Verbal.
96	guile	5.5	not frank	Verbal. Search around for something. I frowned distinctly when it did not come.
97	bully	1.2	fine	Verbal.
98	revel	1.8	rejoice	Verbal.
99	revenge	3.6	vengeance	Verbal. This word scarcely fitted but seemed to be the only one at hand.
100	iniquity	1.1	sin	Verbal.

Observor - D.

No.	Stimulus	Time	Reaction	Introspection
1	arch	3.1	there	"There was a picture of a rounded arch" (The observor failed to give a response, but started to describe the imagery.)
2	prude	3.4	I	"I was looking at your lips ..." (Similar mistake as above) I would have responded with "prune" if I had not failed altogether. I did not think of the meaning of the term but saw the experimentor's lips and thus was suggested "prune".
3	egotism	6.4	I	"I got lost." (Similar mistake) The first thing that came was a visual image of the word, then a confused feeling that I was not giving any response word. I could not get hold of one.
4	single	1.0	double	Visual image of "single" printed and "double" printed below it.
5	chastity	4.0	purity	No imagery. "Purity" given as a definition of "chastity". I felt that I should have responded sooner.
6	ginger	1.1	pepper	Idea that ginger was something to season with and that another seasoning was pepper.
7	shrew	1.0	sugar	I did not get the meaning of the stimulus word until after I had reacted. I was looking at the experimentor's lips and that gave me my cue.
8	adapt	1.2	dentist	It was simple the sound of the word that led to the reaction. I did not get the meaning of the word until afterwards. Visual image of the words after reacting. "Dentist" is a common word in my experience.
9	tough	2.1	nut	Word completion reaction. No visual imagery.
10	morality	1.5	virtue	The meaning which came into my mind was "immorality" and then its opposite "virtue".
11	rubber	2.7	shoe	I was trying to think of something made of rubber and there came a visual image of a rubber overshoe.
12	coquet	1.1	girl	The idea that a coquet is a girl.
13	kick	1.3	kick	I was not sure whether the stimulus was "kit" or "kick" and repeated "kick" as a question. It was not meant to be a reaction.
14	forward	1.3	backward	First was the thot that the experimentor was going to say "formula" as I was looking at him. When I heard "forward", "backward" came, just why I cannot say. After reacting I had

Observor-D.

No.	Stimulus	Time	Reaction	Introspection
14				a visual image of myself going backward. A common conception of myself is one in which I am outside myself and am regarding myself.
15	truth	4.0	honesty	I was confused by watching the lips of the experimentor. Possibly "honesty" came because of the connection that was pointed out in the seminary yesterday, etc.
16	cake	1.1	bread	"Bread" was not the word I wanted. "Pie" was the word. The idea was something to eat. Visual image of two layer cake, etc. No gustatory image.
17	skeptic	7.0	I	"I could not think of a word". (No reaction) The sentence "a man who does not believe" came, but I could not think of a single word. I thought of a discussion that I had just heard along this line.
18	extort	5.0	tort	I was feeling around in my mind for the stimulus word. All I heard was "tort" and there was a tendency to repeat it. I knew that it was not the stimulus word but did not know what came before it.
19	modest	4.4	immodest	I very nearly repeated the stimulus word. I inhibited this because I wanted something else. The reason the stimulus word kept calling for utterance was solely because of the failure of another word to come in.
20	religion	4.8	key hole	At the time the stimulus was given I was practicing giving myself words to see what words came and the stimulus I had just given myself was "key" and the reaction "key hole". The actual stimulus given, tho entirely different from my line of thot did not break it up. I was only conscious that a word had been given and that I had to give a response. I seemed to understand the stimulus word and knew at the time that it was a senseless reaction.
21	knife	1.0	blade	Distinct visual image of a knife and its blade. Word completion idea also present.
22	fanatic	1.2	man	The idea of India came in because of a discussion just previously engaged in. I located the fanatical man in India. No visual imagery.
23	insult	1.4	insane	The sound of the word led to the reaction.

Observor - D.

No.	Stimulus	Time	Reaction	Introspection
24	flaxen	1.4	flatter	Sound reaction. Immediately after reaction the picture of flaxen hair.
25	soul	1.6	sole	This reaction may have been influenced by the fact that the other night I read over a spelling lesson of words pronounced the same but spelled differently. Visual image of "sole" just before reacting.
26	bar	1.0	sky	I was thinking of the sky when the stimulus word was given. I got the stimulus but did not think of its meaning. Of course these reactions are entirely different from the reactions to the same words if met in actual experience of daily life.
27	president	1.0	McKinley	I thot of Taft first, I think. Why I reacted with "McKinley" instead of "Taft" I do not know. Reaction probably of the phrase completion type.
28	fluster	3.8	there	(No reaction) "There was a tendency to repeat the word ...". I forgot to respond and started to give my introspection. I thot of the word as meaning "confuse" after I had inhibited the tendency to repeat it.
29	juicy	.9	juice	Visual image of a liquid. I saw the experimentor say the word and this probably led me to react with the word that I thot was going to be said.
30	death	8.2	it's	(No reaction) "It's gone". I could not associate anything with "death". There was a visual image of a hole in the ground, but it was not a picture of a grave. I meant by "It's gone" that I could not get anything to respond.
31	press	1.9	printing	"Printing" came very quickly, before I could say it. Very clear visual image of a printing press, etc.
32	beauty	2.7	woman	Visual image of the word "beauty". I wanted something that was an illustration. Strain in the throat to say something before I had anything to say.
33	retard	.6	slow	The idea that "retard" means to make go "slow". No imagery.
34	ghostly	1.2	go slow	Sound reaction. (See 33)
35	future	1.2	life	Phrase completion idea and also the feeling of the meaning as something that is going to come.
36	text	1.0	bible	Why I should have thot of "bible" instead of "book" is not clear. There may

Observor - D.

No.	Stimulus	Time	Reaction	Introspection
36				have been vague visual imagery of a verse, or phrase, printed from the Bible.
37	success	3.3	life	The idea of the success of life came and there was a tendency to say "life". I inhibited this because I had responded with life before and I wished a new word. I finally did use it. (See 35)
38	abstract	2.0	abstract	The thing I thot of was not the adjective, but the noun "abstract". Visual image of a certain abstract office.
39	fatalism	1.0	fatal	Sound reaction. In my mind there is connected with the word "fatalism" the idea of death, however, this idea did not occur to me before I reacted. I have a tendency in a good many of these words to repeat the stimulus.
40	gauze	1.4	globe	I was looking at the globe just as the stimulus was given and the "g" sound set it off.
41	error	.8	wrong	Error is something that is wrong. Probably a vague visual image of the word "error". Definition reaction. This tendency to give a definition of a word is very common.
42	gargle	5.3	I	(No reaction) "I stopped it". There was a gurgling sensation in my throat. I was not sure whether the stimulus was "gargle" or "gurgle". I inhibited the tendency to repeat one of these words. The word I finally thot of was "gargoyl".
43	energetic	1.2	energy	Sound reaction.
44	apathy	1.0	ac	I started to react before I had a definite word. It may have been that the word "activity" was intended. It was the sound of the stimulus that set this off.
45	silk	2.8	cloth	I very nearly repeated the stimulus. As I was saying cloth there was a visual image of cloth.
46	stage	6.4	scene	Visual image of a stage. I was trying to think of the name of the wings at the side and could not. The visual image was very clearly defined.
47	curse	1.1	curve	Sound reaction. If I had been thinking of "curse" under ordinary circumstances I would never have thot of "curve".

Observor - D.

No.	Stimulus	Time	Reaction	Introspection
48	duty	5.5	ought	I very nearly repeated the stimulus. While inhibiting this I was definitely conscious of throat strain. The meaning of the stimulus led to the reaction.
49	valor	1.0	vanity	Sound reaction. After reacting the meaning came as bravery.
50	velvet	1.1	cloth	Visual image of black velvet.
51	secure	1.8	safe	Visual image of the word "secure" and a tendency toward the "s" sound. "Safe" was given as a synonym.
52	giggle	1.3	gurgle	The meaning of the stimulus came after the reaction. Sound reaction.
53	inhuman	9.0	I	(No reaction) "I cannot think of any other word". I tried to get a synonym for it. No imagery that I am aware of. The extreme care on the part of the experimentor in annunciating the word distinctly threw me off.
54	ecstacy	1.2	excess	Sound reaction. The word "joy" came immediately afterwards.
55	lace	1.6	late	Sound reaction. There were two things in my mind at the time I said "late". "Late" had no connection with the meaning of the word, but I had a visual image of lace.
56	hint	5.0	lint	When I first thot of "lint" I tried to stop it because it was solely a sound reaction, then I gave way and reacted with it.
57	blush	1.0	bluff	Visual image of a rosy cheek. This image came either before or at the same time as the reaction.
58	wicked	1.2	ricket	I had a visual image of a picket fence. I thot the stimulus was "picket". I have continually tried to get away from these automatic reactions but without success. (At this point the observor determined, still more decidedly not to react solely to the sound of the stimulus.)
59	conscience	1.7	mind	I thot of the meaning of the word "consciousness", altho I understood the stimulus. I nearly reacted with "consciousness". The idea came that consciousness is the mind.
60	shoulder	.8	arm	Visual image of the upper arm and shoulder.
61	graft	1.7	money	Articulatory. I did not think of the real connection between "graft" and "money" until after reacting.
62	behave	1.6	good	"Good" was not the word I wanted. I

Observor - D.

No.	Stimulus	Time	Reaction	Introspection
62				wanted the adverb instead of the adjective. I tried to stop it and get the adverb. Articulatory.
63	sacrifice	1.0	sacred	This came pretty nearly to being an automatic sound reaction. The real meaning of the stimulus word did not come until afterward.
64	philosophy	1.0	philosopher	No imagery.
65	trifle	1.0	little	Definition reaction. No imagery.
66	bedlam	3.1	hord	First there was a tendency to repeat the stimulus. Then the meaning of "bedlam" as "confusion" and a vague visual image of a lot of men.
67	consent	4.5	willingness	(Stop watch stopped - time estimated) I did not hear the stop watch and that confused me. Definition type of reaction.
68	courage	1.0	brave	I should have said "bravery". Definition type.
69	cowardice	.8	brave	"Brave" was more closely associated with "courage" than with this word.
70	course	1.5	rough	(Stimulus taken for "coarse") Visual image of something, I cannot say what, that was rough.
71	habit	2.0	weight	(Stimulus mistaken for "heavy") Visual image of a particular weight.
72	gamble	2.8	gable	Sound reaction. After thinking of "gable" I thot of "money".
73	purity	.9	pure	Automatic sound reaction. At the same time there was the thot that I had been given this word before. (See 5)
74	drug	1.1	drop	Sound reaction. Visual image of the word "drug".
75	snake	.8	snail	Sound reaction. Visual image of both of them.
76	intention	1.8	purpose	Definition reaction.
77	caution	4.9	poison	After I blocked the tendency to repeat the stimulus there came a visual image of a bottle of poison with the word "caution" written in red letters on the label.
78	alimony	.9	alcohol	Sound reaction. I did not think of the meaning of the word until afterwards
79	atheism	2.8	man	I really reacted to "atheist". Definition reaction - an atheist is a man ...
80	cuckoo	.8	clock	Phrase completion reaction, followed by a visual image.
81	height	.7	depth	Kinesthetic tendency to move my eyes upward.
82	deject	4.8	wrong	"Wrong" was not the word I wanted at all.

Observor - D.

No.	Stimulus	Time	Reaction	Introspection
82				I thot more particularly of the adjective "dejected". I do not know why I gave "wrong".
83	concept	1.8	consent	Sound reaction. I did not get the meaning of the stimulus until afterward.
84	temperance	2.0	liquor	Articulatory.
85	chide	2.6	children	Sound reaction. I tried to stop it long enough to think of the meaning, but the meaning did not come and so I let the word go.
86	law	1.7	lawyer	I do not believe that this was altogether and automatic sound reaction because I had in mind the meaning of law and the person connected with it. No visual imagery.
87	virtue	4.0	good	I cannot trace any connection.
88	reverse	1.1	engine	Visual image of the throttle on an engine, etc. Image very clear.
89	handsome	1.0	answer	Sound reaction. I tried to inhibit it but without success.
90	temper	1.4	temperance	Sound reaction. The stimulus seems simply to act as a sort of a trigger to set off a sound similar to it. It is not until after this that I have a clear idea of the meaning of the stimulus. First is simply the idea that I have to react
91	heaven	1.0	God	Articulatory. The idea was that heaven is a place where God is. Visual image of the word "heaven". No tendency to repeat the stimulus.
92	quitter	1.4	man	Tendency to repeat the word or say something like "quick". Then the meaning of the word - a man who quits.
93	thrill	2.0	feeling	Visual image of someone trembling, i.e. being thrilled. Very indistinct.
94	character	2.4	good	The idea was that character may be either good or bad. Articulatory.
95	thief	1.0	theft	Sound reaction. Visual image of a man crawling into a window. I might very appropriately have responded "window".
96	guile	1.4	W. H.	The initials of a man whose name is W.H. Geil. Indistinct visual image of him.
97	bully	2.4	tough	Visual image of a fellow with a bull neck,- a typical "tough."
98	revel	3.0	joy	I nearly repeated the stimulus. I also thot of "rebel". I inhibited this in order to get the meaning of the word. Articulatory.

Observor - D.

No.	Stimulus	Time	Reaction	Introspection
99	revenge	3.7	curse	Articulatory. This must have come from "Reckless Rudolph" in the Chicago Record-Herald.
100	iniquity	1.0	sin	Articulatory. Definition reaction.

Observor - E.

No.	Stimulus	Time	Reaction	Introspection
1	arch	1.7	bow	Visual image of a curve in the shape of a bow. Articulatory repetition of "arch".
2	prude	2.0	Oh	"Oh, I did not get the word". (No reaction) I tried to analize the word and connect it with some other word like "prudence". (The observor is a Japanese student and was not familiar with the word.)
3	egotism	1.2	selfish	One of my instructors used to speak of "egotism and selfishness". I had a visual image of this man, the class, etc.
4	single	1.1	man	Visual image of a man in a big house, all alone, etc. "We live in a sort of double singleness".
5	chastity	1.8	pure	Thot of a play of Shakespere's. The class discussed the characters of the play and the purity of the heroine. Visual image of the page in the book dealing with this.
6	ginger	1.8	salt	Visual image of a bottle of ginger and also a gustatory image of it, which tasted salty.
7	shrew	2.2	wise	(Stimulus mistaken for "shrewd") Visual image of Dean Greene with whom I had a conversation in which he had used the word "shrewd", which was the first time I had heard it, and I learned of its meaning "wise".
8	adapt	2.4	plant	Recently I had a discussion about the adaptability of plants. First was a visual image of the class in which the discussion took place.
9	tough	1.6	beef	I had a kinesthetic image of tough beef and thot of a former dormitory dining room, in visual terms.
10	morality	1.8	man	Same visual image as for "egotism" (3) This instructor said "real manhood is an excellence of morals".
11	rubber	1.4	thief	(Stimulus mistaken for "robber") The two words "robber and thief" go together. My teacher of English used to try and explain the difference in meaning between these two words. Visual image of the class room where the discussion took place etc.
12	coquet	2.2	woman	Visual image of the auditorium stage, where the play "As you like it" was presented a year or two ago. Men took the parts of women and the "woman" next to me said "How coquetish they act". This was the first

Observer - E.

No.	Stimulus	Time	Reaction	Introspection
12				time I had heard the word. It seems that after the stimulus the first thing that comes to my mind is my first experience with that particular English word.
13	kick	1.0	football	Kinesthetic strain in the leg - this indicated "football". Also visual image of the yard where I have kicked a football.
14	forward	1.3	march	I do not take drill. When I heard "forward" it seemed incomplete without adding "march". As soon as I said "forward march" I had a visual image of a play in which the words were used.
15	truth	1.9	God	There is a passage in the Bible "I am the way, the truth,..." This passage was underlined in a Bible that was given me. I had a visual image of this page, the underlining, etc.
16	cake	1.0	eat	Gustatory sensation of sweet and kinesthetic movement of the mouth. No visual imagery.
17	skeptic	1.7	Socrates	Same visual imagery as for "egotism" (3). This instructor explained the Sophists and that they were skeptical of the opinions of others. In connection with this situation "Socrates" came.
18	extort	2.0	face	I connected this word to "distort", which always makes me think of a distorted face. "Distort" came in articulatory terms and then a visual image of a face.
19	modest	1.4	woman	Visual image of a boarding house where we had a social evening. I was asked to speak and spoke about Japanese women and said that they were timid, etc. A lady present said "Japanese women must be very modest". This was my first acquaintance with the word.
20	religion	1.3	Buddha	I recalled a talk which I gave in a church last summer. I spoke about Buddhism and Christianity. Visual image of the church, etc.
21	knife	1.0	sharp	Visual image of a very sharp knife, etc.
22	fanatic	1.4	man	Same visual image as for "egotism" (3). This instructor said, something about like this; "Sometimes men of genius are fanatical". I thot that able men, in one sense, might be

Observor - E.

No.	Stimulus	Time	Reaction	Introspection
22				called fanatical.
23	insult	1.7	person	Visual image of a small house where I used to live. I recalled a discussion "insult" that occurred there. The expression "insult a person" was used.
24	flaxen	1.7	soft	(Stimulus mistaken for "flax") I had a visual image of Japanese flax, which is very soft.
25	soul	2.8	mind	Same visual image as for "egotism". (3) In the class there pictured there was once a discussion of the function of the mind and the soul. The instructor explained the terminology of the words "mind" and "soul" etc
26	bar	1.3	boat	Visual image of a bar at a gate, then of a boat with oars, which are long like the bar at the gate.
27	president	1.0	James	Word completion idea. Articulatory. While reacting I had a visual image of President James, etc.
28	fluster	3.0	stars	I repeated the word for I did not know the meaning. I connected it with another word of similar sound. This word was "cluster". Then a visual image of Professor Stebbins explaining clusters of stars.
29	juicy	2.1	lemon	Visual image of a lemon squeezer full of juice. Also gustatory sensation of lemon.
30	death	1.4	tot	The German word "tot". Visual image of this word in a reader. At one time I was called upon to explain the meaning of "tot" and could not.
31	press	1.4	paper	Visual image of a teacher in English who explained the passage of Franklin's which is something like this: "Fresh from press".
32	beauty	3.0	hat	Visual image of a lady with a long feather in her hat. This is an advertisement of something and the word "beauty" is written in the advertisement.
33	retard	1.2	soldier	I connected the stimulus with the word retired, which led to "retired soldiers". Visual image of retired Japanese soldiers.
34	ghostly	4.0	Kokoro	The name of a book by Lafcadio Hearn. Hearn also wrote "Ghostly Japan". The meaning of Kokoro is not connected with the reaction.
35	future	1.3	heaven	I thot of the phrase "future world" and this lead to the conception of hea-

Observor - E.

No.	Stimulus	Time	Reaction	Introspection
35				ven as the future world. No visual imagery.
36	text	.9	book	Phrase completion. Visual image of Professor Bagley, etc. explaining the uses of a text book.
37	success	2.9	rich man	Visual image of the Success magazine, etc. There was an article in this magazine about a man who was successful in business and who became very rich. Visual image of the man.
38	abstract	1.3	brain	Articulatory. I think of the process of abstracting as an activity of the brain.
39	fatalism	1.2	religion	I thot of the principle of Buddhism, which might be called predestination.
40	gauze	2.4	a bird	I did not know the meaning of the word. I thot of "gosling". I would not have taken this path of association if I had known the word.
41	error	2.8	mathematics	I repeated the stimulus. Visual image of σ = etc. Also visual image of the word "error" as it appeared in a book on statistics.
42	gargle	2.0	throat	Sensation of gargling. Then visual image of a bottle of liquid for gargling.
43	energetic	1.4	iron	Visual image of Sandow, his muscles standing out, etc., with iron dumbbells.
44	apathy	2.1	sympathy	Visual image of the instructor of ethics, etc. It was in this connection that I learned this word for the first time. Sympathy was given as antonym.
45	silk	1.0	soft	Cutaneous sensation of touching yellowish white Japanese silk. Also visual imagery.
46	stage	1.3	theater	Articulatory.
47	curse	1.6	bird	I thot of the German word "flicht" which means something like "curse" and then I thot of "flügel". The derivation of these words was impressed upon me and I established a relation between them. Them the English word "bird".
48	duty	1.3	a man	Visual image of the same teacher. (See 44) He classified the duties of a person (1) to the state, (2) to his family, etc. In this classification the Japanese word for "man" stood out clearly in capitals.

Observor - E.

No.	Stimulus	Time	Reaction	Introspection
49	valor	1.7	brave	"Valor" was an unfamiliar word to me until I studied a certain Shakespere play where the words "bravery" and "valor" occurred together. Visual image of the play, etc.
50	velvet	1.4	soft	Cutaneous sensation and visual image of purple-black velvet, etc.
51	secure	1.4	bank	Yesterday I was looking at a magazine containing a page dealing with securities, investments, etc. A visual image of the page and somewhere on it was the word "bank".
52	giggle	10.0	I	(No reaction) "I had a strange sensation". The stimulus word suggested an act like kicking or striking. Kinesthetic imagery. (Stimulus unfamiliar to the observor).
53	inhuman	1.4	brute	I analyzed the word,separating the "in" from the "human" and in doing so recognized the meaning of it. Then I connected this with "brute".
54	ecstacy	1.3	a man	Visual image of the same teacher (See 44) There occurred to me the fact that a certain philosopher said that he had experienced the state of ecstacy three times in his life. Then a visual image of a man in the clouds, in a halo - my idea of a virtuous man, etc.
55	lace	1.3	horse.	(Stimulus mistaken for "race") Articulatory. I thot of "horse race".
56	hint	1.7	hinder	Sound reaction. Tendency to repeat the stimulus.
57	blush	1.3	cheek	Visual image of a man with red cheeks.
58	wicked	1.4	thief	Visual image of a thief - a Japanese picture, etc. I tried to connect the abstract word with a concrete word representing the same idea.
59	conscience	1.3	mind	The same picture as before (See 44), with a classification in Japanese, etc. Reaction meant as a sort of a definition.
60	shoulder	1.4	a short man	In Othello there is a recitation of Othello's experiences and this led to a visual image of a page of the book and also of a very short man whose head is hidden under his shoulders.
61	graft	1.5	Illinois	A few days ago I was talking about the state legislature. One of the people said "Illinois leads in graft".
62	behave	1.4	woman	Visual image of a Japanese book which was particularly written for young

Observor - E.

No.	Stimulus	Time	Reaction	Introspection
62				women, called, In Japanese, "How to behave".
63	sacrifice	1.8	a man	Visual image of a historic scene - a Japanese general who sacrificed himself for the state, etc.
64	philosophy	1.4	Kant	Visual image of the Japanese instructor who taught elementary philosophy. He was a great admirer of Kant. Indefinite auditory sensation of hearing this man speek about Kant.
65	trifle	1.6	life	I connected "trifle" with "strife", which again is connected with "life." Mere verbal connection due to the sound in the first association. Then indefinite remembrance of a phrase containing both "strife" and "life".
66	bedlam	2.4	chair	(Stimulus mistaken for "bed room") Visual image of a bedroom, etc. ("bedlam" unfamiliar to the observor)
67	consent	1.1	father	In Japan when people marry the consent of the father must be obtained. First was the idea of marriage and then of the person who gives consent.
68	courage	2.0	vigorous	Visual image of a strong man, perhaps Sandow. I connected this with vigorousness.
69	cowardice	1.4	river	"Kawa" in Japanese means river. Sound reaction. Visual image of a river etc.
70	course	2.0	cloud	Thot of the class in German this morning in which we read of the charcoal burner seeing a "course of clouds".
71	habit	2.7	form	Visual image of Professor Bagley. He recommended a book on "Habit formation".
72	gamble	1.8	checkers	Visual image of a group of people gambling, as pictured at a moving picture show. They seemed to be playing a sort of checkers.
73	purity	.9	virtue	Articulatory. No particular meaning in the reaction.
74	drug	2.3	a root	This again is from the German class this morning. There appeared the statement by Joan of Arc that she knows roots and herbs as medicine.
75	snake	2.3	coil	Visual image of a snake coiled up, etc.
76	intention	2.2	attention	Sound reaction.
77	caution	2.0	an old man	In Japan it is a by word that "an old man is always over cautious".
78	alimony	2.0	fruit	(Stimulus unfamiliar to the observor) I thot of "almond." ("l" pronounced)

Observor - E.

No.	Stimulus	Time	Reaction	Introspection
79	atheism	1.9	picture	I connect "atheism" with the French revolution and the cult of reason. I imageined all orthodox faiths leaving and the cult of reason taking their place. I had a vague visual image of a picture, or figure representing "reason".
80	cuckoo	1.3	bird	Visual image of a bird and an auditory image of the sad note of a bird.
81	height	2.7	place	I thot of "high place". Phrase completion. Visual image of a plateau, etc.
82	deject	2.4	food	(Stimulus mistaken for "digest") First was the articulatory repetition of the stimulus, then I thot of a lecture concerning the digestion of plants - their means of taking in food, etc.
83	concept	1.1	parent	(Stimulus mistaken for "consent") Thot of the consent of parents when people marry. No visual imagery.
84	temperance	3.7	sanguine	(Stimulus mistaken for "temperament") Articulatory. Thot of a classification of temperaments, one of which was "sanguine".
85	chide	2.9	childish	I did not know the meaning of "chide" and the reaction was due to the similarity of sound.
86	bedlam	1.5	government	Articulatory. Some such phrase as "law and government" seemed to be present.
87	virtue	2.5	purity	In Japanese there is a phrase "purity is virtue". I thot of this phrase.
88	reverse	1.5	pole	Visual image of Professor Bagley, who spoke of "attention" and "habit" as being at the ends of a pole. I thot of the reversed or opposite positions of "attention" and "habit" on this pole.
89	handsome	1.8	man	Articulatory. I drew a distinction between the words "beautiful" and "handsome", thinking of "beautiful woman" and "handsome man".
90	temper	2.2	angry	Thot of the phrase "man of temper" and of being told that this meant a hot dispositioned man. Articulatory.
91	heaven	1.3	cloud	Visual image of the sky with clouds floating and with beams of light, etc.
92	quitter	6.0	truant	Articulatory. First there was hesitation because I was unfamiliar with the word "quitter", tho familiar

Observor - E.

No.	Stimulus	Time	Reaction	Introspection
92				with "quit". I constructed the word "quitter" as "one who quits", before any other associations came. Then I thot of the school boy who plays hookey.
93	thrill	2.0	string	I connected "thrill" with the trembling motions of the strings of pianos. Distinct visual image of the steel strings of a piano.
94	character	1.9	dignified person	Thot of the phrase "man of character" and then had a clear visual image of a dignified man, etc.
95	thief	2.1	bad	Articulatory. I tried to distinguish "thief" from "robber" and to analyse these characters and the activity of each.
96	guile	2.2	guilt	I did not know the meaning of "guile" and reacted due to the similarity of sound and of spelling. First was an articulatory repetition of the stimulus and an attempt to connect the word with something like "seagull". This attempt was dropped.
97	bully	2.7	a little girl	I know of a certain little girl who says "bully" upon all occasions. Visual image of her.
98	revel	3.7	scale	(Stimulus mistaken for "level") I thot of a level and reacted with "scale" because it is something that is in equilibrium, that is level. Visual image of a pair of scales with two pans. The mistake in the stimulus is probably due to the universal fact that Japanese find it difficult to distinguish between "l" and "r".
99	revenge	1.3	dagger	Visual image of a fierce looking person with a dagger and ready to thrust.
100	iniquity	2.7	French revolution	I understood the pronunciation of the stimulus word, but thot of it as being the same as "inequality". I heard "inequality" for the first time in connection with the French revolution, where the inequality in wealth was given as the prime cause for the revolution.

Observor - F.

No.	Stimulus	Time	Reaction	Introspection
1	arch	1.4	dome	Visual image of an arch, which expanded until it became a dome.
2	prude	7.0	---	(No reaction) I kept wondering whether I understood the word correctly. There was a groping around.
3	egotism	1.9	man	Thot of a certain man, whom I think of as being egotistical. There was first a visual image of a man - this later became this particular man.
4	single	1.1	double	I thot of "single" as being applied to an unmarried man. I seemed to see the sentence "A single man". Then I thot of double as being the opposite of single. The visual imagery was indistinct at first.
5	chastity	1.4	virtue	I thot that "chastity" was like "virtue" and also that "virtue" was on the list previously worked with. In this connection I had a visual image of the laboratory room, etc.
6	ginger	1.6	cooky	Word completion type of reaction. A hazy visual image.
7	shrew	1.3	taming...	"Taming of the shrew". Visual image of a part of the play. No phrase completion idea.
8	adapt	1.5	adaptation	Word completion idea. No visual imagery. Thot of adaptation as applied in biology.
9	tough	1.7	knot	Thot of a knot such as a tough pine knot. Hazy visual image of a knot on a piece of wood.
10	morality	3.0	preacher	Visual image of a man standing up in a pulpit talking about morality.
11	rubber	1.2	ball	Visual image of a rubber ball. Possibly partly a word completion reaction.
12	coquet	2.2	girl	Visual image of a girl of the type of a dark haired French maid, etc.
13	kick	2.7	ball	Visual image of a young man kicking. The visual idea came considerably before the word ball.
14	forward	2.2	march	Word completion reaction. No visual imagery.
15	truth	3.2	application	Thot of the expression that is very common in scientific writings, "the application of this truth...".
16	cake	2.6	hole	Visual image of an old fashioned cake with a hole in the center.
17	skeptic	1.2	man	Thot of skepticism as being a quality of man's nature.
18	extort	6.0	Paris	Thot of the French revolution when the noblemen were extorting things from the peasants. This centered about Paris.

Observor - F.

No.	Stimulus	Time	Reaction	Introspection
19	modest	1.2	girl	Visual image of a sweet sixteen girl.
20	religion	1.4	church	Simply the idea of connection between religion and churches. Hazy visual image of a body of people worshipping.
21	knife	1.0	sharp	Visual image of a knife. Another word came just about the same time as "sharp". This was "cut".
22	fanatic	5.6	boy	Considerably before I reacted I thot of an occasion when the word was mispronounced by a boy and called "fanátic". It was the thot of this boy that led to the reaction. There was a strong tendency to say "fanátic".
23	insult	2.9	man	Hazy visual image of a man coming along the street shoving over to one side a lady.
24	flaxen	1.6	hair	Visual image of a head of flaxen hair.
25	soul	1.6	foot	Thot of the "sole of the foot". Phrase completion reaction.
26	bar	1.9	standing...	"Standing at the bar". Visual image of a row of men standing at the bar all with one foot up on the rod, etc. The expression came complete in itself.
27	president	1.3	McKinley	I do not know why McKinley came as representing one of the presidents of the United States. Partly of the phrase completion type of reaction.
28	fluster	1.5	flustrate	I thot of one having stage fright being all in a fluster - being "flustrated"
29	juicy	1.2	pear	Visual image of a pear, etc.
30	death	3.6	man	Thot of death coming to man. No visual imagery.
31	press	1.8	printing	Visual image of a small printing press.
32	beauty	1.3	girl	Visual image of a pretty girl.
33	retard	1.4	bed	(Stimulus mistaken for "retire") The expression "go to bed" occurred to me. No visual imagery.
34	ghostly	3.0	spirit	Thot of the connection between "ghosts and spirits". No distinct visual imagery.
35	future	1.2	happiness	Phrase completion reaction.
36	text	1.0	book	Phrase completion.
37	success	1.0	future	Association of the ideas "future and success" with probably a little of

Observor - F.

No.	Stimulus	Time	Reaction	Introspection
37				the phrase completion idea.
38	abstract	1.8	deed	Thot of as synonymous. Also visual image of a certain abstract office.
39	fatalism	1.7	death	No visual imagery. Thot of fatalists and the way in which they look forward to death.
40	gauze	1.3	wire	Phrase completion.
41	error	1.0	mistake	Synonym. Later a visual image. In all of these reactions I get later considerable visual imagery.
42	gargle	1.2	throat	Thot of myself as gargling and having sore throat. Visual with possibly a little kinesthetic imagery.
43	energetic	1.4	strong	Visual image of an athlete, showing the muscles tense.
44	apathy	2.9	tired	Hazy visual image of a person lying down appearing to be all worn out.
45	silk	1.0	dress	Visual image of a black silk dress.
46	stage	.8	fright	Phrase completion.
47	curse	.9	swear	Simultaneous visual and auditory image of a man swearing. The man was in a rage, etc. Altho I could hear him I do not remember the particular expressions that he used.
48	duty	5.5	help	Repetition of stimulus to myself. The idea was that one's duty is to help. I was unaware of this repetition of the stimulus word at the time I did it, and became aware that I had done so later.
49	valor	1.0	bravery	Articulatory. Similar ideas.
50	velvet	1.3	soft	Visual image of a small piece of black velvet, together with the cutaneous sensation of softness.
51	secure	1.0	help	Articulatory. The idea seemed to be that when one is making someone else secure they are helping them.
52	giggle	1.4	girl	Sound reaction. Quite meaningless at the time of reaction.
53	inhuman	1.4	beastly	Synonym. There was the thot of the French revolution in vague visual imagery, similar to the previous reaction. (See 18).
54	ecstacy	1.1	happiness	Articulatory.
55	lace	2.0	feather	This came from the expression "feathers and fine lace".
56	hint	1.4	talk	Articulatory. There is a connection between these words, but it is hard

Observor - F.

No.	Stimulus	Time	Reaction	Introspection
56				to explain. One drops a hint while talking.
57	blush	1.0	shame	At least partly phrase completion - "blush for shame".
58	wicked	1.4	bad	Articulatory. Synonym.
59	conscience	1.6	mind	Articulatory. From "conscience" I thot of "consciousness", due to the similarity of sound. This suggested the word "mind".
60	shoulder	1.3	blade	Phrase completion.
61	graft	1.8	mean	Articulatory. The idea of a grafter being a mean man.
62	behave	1.2	act	Articulatory. Similarity in meaning.
63	sacrifice	1.3	altar	Indistinct visual image of someone offerring up a sacrifice on an altar.
64	philosophy	1.4	psychology	Partly articulatory and partly visual. Thot of a discussion concerning philosophy and connected this with the department of psychology. Visual image of the place where the discussion took place and of some of the men.
65	trifle	1.0	little	Articulatory.
66	bedlam	2.1	loose	I did not quite get the word at first. Thot of the expression "bedlam broke loose". Articulatory.
67	consent	2.0	hesitate	Vague visual image of two fellows talking and one trying to get the other to consent to something - the second fellow hesitated.
68	courage	1.2	bravery	Articulatory.
69	cowardice	1.4	courage	Articulatory. This brought the previous reaction to mind.
70	course	1.0	fine	(Stimulus taken for "coarse") Articulatory. Antonym.
71	habit	2.7	mind	Articulatory. Thot of habit as applied to one's mental processes.
72	gamble	1.5	spend	Articulatory. Thot of one who gambles as a spendthrift. Very faint visual imagery of such a place as Monte Carlo.
73	purity	1.3	vice	Articulatory. Contrast idea.
74	drug	1.5	store	Phrase completion. Just about the same time I thot of a particular situation that occurred this morning.
75	snake	1.3	crawl	Visual image of a snake crawling.
76	intention	1.2	purpose	Articulatory. Synonym.

Observor - F.

No.	Stimulus	Time	Reaction	Introspection.
77	caution	1.6	purpose	The connection is vague and the reaction word came because of its use immediately preceding. The idea seemed to be that when one cautions another they have some purpose in mind.
78	alimony	1.6	marriage	Visual image of notices in the newspapers of marriage, divorce and alimony.
79	atheism	1.8	dogmatism	Articulatory. A whole jumble of ideas came immediately. Among them the idea that atheist is most strongly opposed by the dogmatic narrow minded Christian.
80	cuckoo	1.0	bill	There are two kinds of cuckoos. They are distinguished by their bills. Faint visual image of a bird. Later of a clock.
81	height	.8	black	(Stimulus mistaken for "white") Contrast idea. No visual imagery.
82	deject	2.2	poor	Partly phrase completion - "poor and dejected", together with the idea of poverty causing the dejection.
83	concept	1.6	idea	Articulatory. Similarity of meaning.
84	temperance	1.7	intemperance	Articulatory. Contrast.
85	chide	1.2	upbraid	Articulatory.
86	law	1.7	medicine	Partly phrase completion - "law and medicine". Faintly auditory, hearing the same phrase.
87	virtue	1.3	vice	Articulatory. Contrast.
88	reverse	1.1	opposite	Articulatory.
89	handsome	1.0	pleasant	Articulatory. The idea of handsomeness and pleasantness being combined, applied to people.
90	temper	1.8	mean	Phrase completion, inverted. A "mean temper".
91	heaven	1.1	hell	Articulatory. Idea of contrast. Partly phrase completion - "heaven and hell".
92	quitter	1.5	stop	Articulatory. A quitter is one who stops.
93	thrill	3.8	help.	The idea was that when one attempts to do anything and does accomplish it he has a thrill of pleasure and that this is a help to further accomplishment.
94	character	1.3	habit	Thot of one's character being but a bundle of habits.
95	thief	1.1	steal	Articulatory. Thot of a thief's actions.

Observor - F.

No.	Stimulus	Time	Reaction	Introspection
96	guile	2.0	simple	Thot of one who is without guile as being a simple person.
97	bully	1.2	coward	Articulatory. Partly phrase completion idea. Thot of these two qualities as going together.
98	revel	1.3	revelry	Word completion. Thot of the battle of Waterloo and the revelry of the night before the battle. Faint visual imagery. (See 18 and 53)
99	revenge	1.2	anger	Articulatory. When one takes revenge he is always angry.
100	iniquity	1.0	sin	Partly phrase completion, inverted - "sin and iniquity". Very vague visual-auditory image of a minister preaching.

Observor - G.

No.	Stimulus	Time	Reaction	Introspection
1	arch	2.0	arc de...	"Arc de Triumph". A visual image of it
2	prude	1.2	woman	Visual image of a young Puritan woman.
3	egotism	1.4	E. A. ...	Visual image of a man whose initials are E. A. and who was nicknamed "Ego A.
4	single	2.0	matrimony	A train of thots and visual images, very brief and ephemeral. Thot of a single man, then a particular marriage license, a house, a yard and finally the reaction.
5	chastity	1.3	woman	No visual imagery. I thot of a conversation in which "virtue "and "woman " were associated.
6	ginger	1.5	ginger bread	Visual image of "Huyler's Ginger Root" but "ginger bread" came first. Phrase completion reaction.
7	shrew	1.8	woman	Vague memory of colonial manner of treating the shrew, as pictured in Barn's History. No visual imagery.
8	adapt	2.4	Darwin	Visual image of my book shelf at home, with Darwin's book on it.
9	tough	1.5	alley	Visual image of a ruffian in an alley.
10	morality	1.2	woman	No visual imagery. No explanation.
11	rubber	1.3	Panama	Visual image of a rubber forest located in South America, but could not readily say "South America" so switched to "Panama".
12	coquet	1.0	woman	Visual image of a young lady.
13	kick	1.0	horse	Visual image of a barn and stall, as it appears upon first entering. No visual image of horse.
14	forward	2.4	excelsior	Visual image of a boy climbing up a mountain, with a flag, etc.
15	truth	10.0	Lincoln	Visual image of Thaddeus Stevens being carried into Congress to make a speech, etc. There was no word to express this. Then I said "Oh shaw" and started again to find a word. "Lincoln "was associated with reconstruction times. The reason why I started with a visual image of Thaddeus Stevens is problematical. Possibly my reading about the Lorimer case and the lack of truth in Congress led me to think of Congress and the rest.
16	cake	1.4	German	Visual image of German cake, etc. and then the cake placed itself in the hands of a German woman.
17	skeptic	1.9	Brown	Visual image of an old man, etc. whose name is Brown. Before this I had

Observor - G.

No.	Stimulus	Time	Reaction	Introspection
17				the thot of such characters as Ingersol, etc. and they finally took the form of this old man.
18	extort	1.4	Chicago	Visual image of the inside of a house of prostitution. I believe this came from reading quite recently of extortion by politicians from this type of people.
19	modest	.9	woman	Visual image of a woman wearing a veil.
20	religion	1.2	Bode	Visual image of Professor Bode. I took a course in the philosophy of religion under him.
21	knife	.9	cut	No image.
22	fanatic	1.3	Dervisher	Visual image of Sudan, associated with Kipling's "Fuzzy Wuzzy".
23	insult	1.6	boy	Visual image of a man with his hat knocked off. No apparent connection between this picture and "boy."
24	flaxen	1.2	farm	Visual image of flax farm in Minnesota.
25	soul	1.7	religion	No imagery. No explanation - there was a train of thot that I cannot trace.
26	bar	2.0	Brown	Visual image of a saloon bar, etc. The "Brown" in the reaction was Lee O'Niel Brown.
27	president	1.0	McKinley	Visual image of McKinley. The reason I thot of McKinley instead of Taft is probably because I recently read of a person canvassing "The life of McKinley".
28	fluster	.9	woman	Visual image of a woman trying to find the pocket in her skirt. Sometime ago I saw a cartoon picturing this.
29	juicy	1.0	orange	Visual image of an orange grove. Combatting this picture was that of an orange crushed up and the juice running out.
30	death	1.3	grand mother	Visual image of a person on her death bed.
31	press	1.0	orange	No visual image. (See 29 for possible explanation)
32	beauty	.8	woman	Visual image of a woman.
33	retard	1.2	stop	No image.
34	ghostly	1.0	ghost	Visual image of a ghost - a white apparition with a hood drawn over its head, etc.
35	future	2.9	coming	Just a feeling of futurity; something potential impending; of blank space. I wanted to repeat the stimulus as best expressing the feeling.

Observor - G.

No.	Stimulus	Time	Reaction	Introspection
36	text	.6	book	Visual image of a green arithmetic.
37	success	1.0	magazine	Visual image of the Success Magazine. No word completion idea.
38	abstract	1.0	book	Visual image of an abstract, but I could not think of the word "dosier" which I wanted so I called it "book."
39	fatalism	1.2	Arabian	Visual image of a Mohammedan dressed in white. I could not think of Mohammedan so took the next term Arabian
40	gauze	1.0	cloth	Visual image of gauze cloth.
41	error	.8	book	I have been correcting proof for a book. No visual imagery.
42	gargle	1.1	throat	Visual image of a throat. No kinesthetic imagery.
43	energetic	.8	work	Visual image of myself mixing concrete. No kinesthetic imagery.
44	apathy	1.0	disgust	No visual image, Sort of a feeling of pushing something away. No kinesthetic imagery, rather a mental push.
45	silk	.7	rustle	Vague visual image of a silk skirt. Auditory image of rustling probably stronger than the visual image.
46	stage	.8	hand	Phrase completion. Visual image of a stage coach.
47	curse	.7	swear	No imagery unless possibly very vague visual image of someone swearing.
48	duty	1.0	soldier	The phrase "honor is duty" ran thru my head before the term soldier came.
49	valor	1.1	soldier	No imagery.
50	velvet	2.0	soft	Sort of a cutaneous feeling, followed by a visual image.
51	secure	.7	safe	Visual image of the Rock of Gibraltar.
52	giggle	1.6	giggle	I started to ask if "giggle" was the stimulus. I was caught thinking about the force of advertising, particularly the advertisement using the Rock of Gibralter in it. (51)
53	inhuman	1.3	shoot	Vague visual image of a man beating a horse. I think I tried to say "hit" before I reacted with "shoot".
54	ecstacy	.8	joy	No imagery. I used to have a friend who used the expression "Oh joy, oh ecstacy", tho I did not think of this fact until after reacting.
55	lace	.7	dress	Visual image of a lace petticoat.
56	hint	.9	suggestion	Thot of a person hinting. No visual imagery.
57	blush	1.0	red	Visual image of a girl blushing.

Observor - G.

No.	Stimulus	Time	Reaction	Introspection
58	wicked	.7	bad	No imagery.
59	conscience	1.9	Sidis	Altho I heard the stimulus very well I confused it with "conscious". The idea of the subconscious came in my mind and the book by Sidis which I had just been reading.
60	shoulder	1.6	coat	Visual image of someone shrugging one shoulder, in which act the coat stood out distinctly.
61	graft	1.0	orange	Visual image of a young orange tree that had been grafted.
62	behave	1.1	mind ...	"Mind your business." Visual image of a woman slapping a child.
63	sacrifice	1.0	slaughter	Visual image of a Greek place of offering.
64	philosophy	.6	Bode	No imagery.
65	trifle	.9	small	No imagery.
66	bedlam	.8	mixture	Visual image of an insane asylum. A rather vague picture.
67	consent	1.2	woman	I thot of statutes governing age of consent. No visual imagery.
68	courage	1.7	red badge	Visual image of the book "Red badge of courage".
69	cowardice	1.4	run	Visual image of a Union soldier running thru the woods.
70	course	1.1	run	Visual image of a small creek.
71	habit	2.0	smoking	No picture. Thot of the difficulty in breaking a habit.
72	gamble	1.6	O'Leary	Visual image of a typical gambler - O'Leary.
73	purity	1.7	Puritan	Visual image of a Puritan woman.
74	drug	1.5	opium	Visual image of a drug clerk pouring out drugs, etc.
75	snake	.8	grass	Visual image of a snake sticking its head out of some wiry grass.
76	intention	1.3	marry	Visual image of a certain old lady who used to wonder if I had any serious intentions in regard to a girl in her charge.
77	caution	1.4	railroad	Visual image of a locomotive.
78	alimony	1.4	pay up	Visual image of a picture in the Record Herald and an article, "Shall the rich wives pay alimony?"
79	atheism	2.0	Bode	No imagery.
80	cuckoo	.8	cuckoo clock	Visual image of a clock, etc. The image was very clear.
81	height	1.9	Waterloo	I was just thinking of Waterloo. When

Observor - G.

No.	Stimulus	Time	Reaction	Introspection
81				I heard "height" I thot of Napoleon, etc.
82	deject	1.4	reject	No imagery.
83	concept	1.4	sketch	No imagery.
84	temperance	.8	drink	Visual image of an old woman associated with a glass of beer. My grand-mother was a temperance worker.
85	chide	1.7	criticise	I mistook the word at first and thot it was "child". Then I realized that it was "chide" and thot of chiding a child. Visual image of the child.
86	law	1.3	law book	Visual image of a book of statutes. It is not likely there was any of the phrase completion idea.
87	virtue	1.5	woman	No imagery.
88	reverse	.9	engine	Visual image of the reverse lever on an engine.
89	handsome	.6	man	Phrase completion idea. Visual image came afterwards.
90	temper	1.2	angry	Visual image of a certain man who gets angry rather easily.
91	heaven	1.1	gate	Visual image of the blue sky. No image of a gate.
92	quitter	.7	animal	(Stimulus mistaken for "crittur") No imagery.
93	thrill	.8	feeling	Visual image of a theater, etc., with a thrilling melodramatic scene.
94	character	1.1	boy	Visual image of a young man. Probably this came because this morning I had occasion to make some mental comments on young men's character.
95	thief	.6	run	Visual image of a man running.
96	guile	1.0	craft	Visual image of a snake. "Craft" taken in the sense of "crafty".
97	bully	1.2	Theodore	Visual image of Roosevelt.
98	revel	2.1	rebel	I misunderstood the word at the start and thot of "rebel". When the word became clear I thot of a revel - a dance.
99	revenge	.6	anger	No imagery.
100	iniquity	1.4	sin	Sort of a vague image of the walls of Jerusalem.

Observor - H.

No.	Stimulus	Time	Reaction	Introspection
1	arch	1.7	stone	Visual image of a curved arch with a segment of stone.
2	prude	1.8	tried	(Mistook the stimulus for "prove") Faint visual image of a court room, which suggested "tried".
3	egotism	2.2	I	Thot of my own egotism. No visual imagery. I thot of myself first as away from myself and then approaching and becoming one with me.
4	single	1.6	married	Weak visual imagery of a young man and then a young women, both single, - then married. Kinesthetic sensations color the entire experience. The visual is the core of it and the kinesthetic is of the nature of a general feeling in the matter. When I have a visual image of a man moving, connected with it are the kinesthetic sensations of myself moving. When, in the image above the young man reached out toward the girl with his hand I felt myself doing the same.
5	chastity	2.0	virgin	Visual image of a girl having a very white face - "white as a lily".
6	ginger	2.3	ade	"Ale" was what I meant. Visual image of a bottle.
7	shrew	1.5	false	(Mistook the stimulus for "true") Vague visual image and kinesthetic image of writing with the hand. The visual image was an image of script. It seemed as tho I were writing the stimulus word.
8	adapt	2.6	myself	Thot of "adapt" as a question - adapt what? - myself. Articulatory. After thinking of this I hesitated sometime before reacting.
9	tough	1.6	pull	After the stimulus there was the sensation of looking for something - feeling of mal-adjustment. Then a kinesthetic sensation of pulling something apart and finally a visual image of the experimentor doing this.
10	morality	1.3	true	Association untraceable. I have used these words together a great many times.
11	rubber	1.0	neck	Phrase completion reaction.
12	coquet	1.2	girl	Faint visual image of a girl.
13	kick	1.1	mule	Visual image of a mule kicking and the feeling of myself getting out of the way.

Observor - H.

No.	Stimulus	Time	Reaction	Introspection
14	forward	1.4	go	Kinesthetic feeling of leaning forward, which means to go.
15	truth	1.4	righteous-ness	Articulatory.. There was a general feeling about the body suggesting truth, something like the way one feels when in church. There is a certain halo, not visual, about the word "truth" that suggests another word with a similar halo.
16	cake	1.2	eat	Faint visual image, together with the feeling in the mouth, of eating.
17	skeptic	1.4	man	In looking for an association word by repeating the stimulus I went thru such a process as this: skeptic, skeptical man, man. Articulatory.
18	extort	1.2	money	I had my hand in my pocket on some money. I seemed to be pulling money out of somebody's pocket. Kinesthetic, with slight visual imagery of the other person.
19	modest	1.2	girl	Same sort of an association as (8) and (15). Modest - modest what? - modest girl. The general feeling that goes with "modest", which is the same as that which goes with "girl".
20	religion	1.3	bible	Articulatory. I cannot trace the association in any way.
21	knife	.9	cut	Visual image of a knife blade cutting a pencil toward me, my finger being in the way. Kinesthetic feeling of pulling the finger away and also of pulling the knife. "Cut" comes from thinking of my finger being cut
22	fanatic	1.7	man	Articulatory. The general feeling of something to get away from. While I was inclined to get away from the fanatic I was at the same time trying to observe and describe him.
23	insult	2.0	hit	The reaction word followed a feeling of bodily adjustment of warding off something. Faint visual image of a man and the impulse to hit him.
24	flaxen	1.7	headed	Visual image of a tow headed girl. Articulatory and visual - the articulatory comes in in the effort to say something.
25	soul	1.0	body	Purely articulatory. No thinking necessary to get these words together.
26	bar	1.4	beer	Visual image of a bar. Kinesthetic feeling of holding onto the railing of the bar. "Beer" comes as something to be expected. Visual image very definite.

Observor - H.

No.	Stimulus	Time	Reaction	Introspection
27	president	1.4	Taft	Visual image of Taft just about as I said the word. Otherwise my mind was blank.
28	fluster	1.4	hurry	General kinesthetic and nervous feeling all over the body giving rise to the articulatory impulse to say "hurry".
29	juicy	1.7	mellow	Kinesthetic feeling in the mouth, etc. Faint visual image of a muskmelon.
30	death	4.0	no	(No reaction) "No reaction to that". My mind was diverted. I heard the word but it had no significance.
31	press	1.4	press	I was not sure of the stimulus. There was simply a large question as to what it was all about. This is the usual attitude at the beginning when any stimulus word is given.
32	beauty	1.2	girl	I found myself searching for a "beauty." Faint visual image of a blond girl.
33	retard	1.3	stop	Articulatory combined with kinesthetic feeling. There was the idea of retarding more and more until there was a complete stop. I located this indefinitely in my right arm, probably because I play the violin. No visual imagery.
34	ghostly	1.2	ghastly	Visual image of a ghost. Articulatory repetition of the stimulus which suggested "ghastly". The general complex appropriate to ghosts contains "ghastly". The visual image was of a white sheeted person, the face very vague. The response was with a sort of a sarcastic idea.
35	future	1.2	time	No visual imagery. "Future" brought up the idea of "future what?" and the answer "future time". A Phrase completion reaction.
36	text	.9	book	Faint visual image of a book. I felt myself reaching for it. Phrase completion reaction.
37	success	6.6	I	(No reaction) "I can't think of any association". There was about as blank a feeling as I have ever had. Felt like being on the stage and forgetting my speech.
38	abstract	.7	term	I wanted to connect abstract with something. There seemed the necessity of completing the idea, - "abstract term".
39	fatalism	1.8	philosophy	Visual image of the word "fatalism" printed as tho a chapter heading. It was a philosophy book.

Observpr - H.

No.	Stimulus	Time	Reaction	Introspection
40	gauze	1.0	thin	I saw thru a white gauze veil and felt it with my fingers.
41	error	1.7	mistake	For quite a long time the stimulus word did not seem to arouse anything in my mind. Finally the attempt was to tell the significance of it.
42	gargle	1.3	throat	The experience was that of gargling. Kinesthetic with slight visual imagery.
43	energetic	1.1	hasty	This aroused the general feeling of getting busy. No visual imagery.
44	apathy	1.2	deadness	Felt myself sitting in the chair, feeling dead. "Apathy" suggested myself at once.
45	silk	1.7	gauze	This was connected with the reaction for "gauze". (See 40) Visual image of silk, etc.
46	stage	1.4	actor	Visual image of an actor on the stage, etc. No kinesthetic feeling.
47	curse	.9	swear	Articulatory. I tried to get a synonym.
48	duty	3.9	do it	These words were suggested immediately, but I hesitated to say them. Articulatory repetition of the word made it easy to react as I did. The very word "duty" implies "do it".
49	valor	1.4	bravery	Visual image of a knight riding on horse back, etc. There was the feeling that goes with valor and bravery.
50	velvet	2.2	pillow	Faint visual image of a piece of black velvet and I also had the cutaneous sensation of feeling it. Then I attempted to discover the shape of the velvet and it became a pillow.
51	secure	1.7	fasten	"Fast" was the first word that came. Articulatory and some kinesthetic feeling of being secured and straining against the bonds.
52	giggle	.9	girl	Faint visual image of a girl giggling. Kinesthetic sensation of feeling nervous, which is the sensation I have when I hear someone giggling.
53	inhuman	1.4	brute	I said "dog" to myself but this did not pop out. I tried to complete the idea "inhuman what?". "Dog" did not fit the situation. Just a flash of a visual image of a dog.
54	ecstacy	1.4	delight	Feeling of ecstacy. "Delight" comes up out of this general background.
55	lace	.9	tight	The words went together "lace tight" and the idea that of a woman lacing tight. Faint visual image of a

Observor - H.

No.	Stimulus	Time	Reaction	Introspection
55				woman pulling her corset strings tight.
56	hint	.9	suggestion	The echo of the experimentor's voice continued for a slight length of time. No articulatory imagery.
57	blush	1.7	woman	Predicate type of reaction. I experienced the feeling of uneasiness which I experience when I see a person blushing. Faint visual image of a woman with red cheeks.
58	wicked	1.6	boy	Predicate type. "Wicked what? - boy." The same feeling that goes with "wicked" goes with the object to which it is attached.
59	conscience	1.4	pain	The feeling of "conscience" is something which pricks, - pain. "Conscience" suggests some sort of an inner feeling and this idea is closely connected with the idea of "pain".
60	shoulder	1.0	blade	Visual image of a man's shoulder, looking from behind, with the shoulder blade very prominent. The visual imagery seems to be the medium thru which I reached "blade".
61	graft	1.0	corruption	These words feel the same. Practically synonyms.
62	behave	1.4	splendid	Articulatory. The sound of "s" came and I completed the word from this beginning. Purely an accidental association. I have no idea why the sound of "s" should have come.
63	sacrifice	2.3	money	Articulatory. "Sacrifice what? - money". Felt the tendency to have visual imagery, but I did not get any.
64	philosophy	1.6	time	A "mood"/association. I think of philosophy as something that moves slowly and time has the same general significance.
65	trifle	1.0	play	The feeling of "trifle" is the same as that of "full of play".
66	bedlam	1.1	noise	A general "feeling" association. "Bedlam" is something that is disagreeable, as is a "big noise". Indistinct visual image of a broom stick flying out the door of a room.
67	consent	1.0	will	Possibly a little articulatory imagery. "Consent" has the same feeling about it that "will" has. These words seem to have the same fringe and the fringe is the medium of association.
68	courage	1.3	brave	General similarity of feeling about the words.

Observor - H.

No.	Stimulus	Time	Reaction	Introspection
69	cowardice	1.4	run	Kinesthetic association. Faint visual image of a Greek running away, etc. I had the general bodily feeling of turning away from something.
70	course	1.7	way	Visual image of a particular race track. I was more interested in the track than to reacting and "way" was given rather absent-mindedly. "Track" would have been a better word.
71	habit	1.1	garret	(Stimulus mistaken for "attic") General bodily feeling that is the same with both of these words.
72	gamble	1.0	play	Kinesthetic feeling of throwing cards down upon the table. Slight visual imagery of cards.
73	purity	1.2	virginity	General "mood" feeling. No visual or articulatory imagery.
74	drug	1.1	man	(Stimulus mistaken for "drunk") Faint visual image of a man who was drunk and the feeling of sympathy for him.
75	snake	1.3	bite	Faint visual image of a snake and the feeling of drawing the hand back to prevent the snake from biting it. The kinesthetic feeling predominated.
76	intention	1.6	do	The feeling of intending to do something. A general forward feeling of the body. No visual or articulatory imagery.
77	caution	1.5	don't	Before I said "don't" I said "do" very faintly in inner speech. (See 76) It was as if I had been commanded to caution someone and was saying to him "don't ...". Kinesthetic verbal association.
78	alimony	1.0	marriage	No explanation further than that these words have the same general tone.
79	atheism	.9	God	General kinesthetic feeling. I think of atheism as opposition to God.
80	cuckoo	1.0	dove	Visual image of a white dove. This image seemed to be responsible for the reaction word.
81	height	1.0	dream	(Stimulus mistaken for "pipe") Phrase completion "pipe dream", together with the feeling of enjoying one, etc.
82	deject	1.7	cast down	No imagery apparent. The word "deject" has a certain atmosphere and when this atmosphere is experienced another word with the same fringe, or atmosphere, comes up. Kinesthetic feeling would seem to be the path of association.

Observor - H.

No.	Stimulus	Time	Reaction	Introspection
83	concept	1.4	word	First a definite attempt to apperceive the stimulus word. After getting it "word" came out of the same general complex.
84	temperance	1.4	beer	Whenever I think of temperance I think of what it opposes, there is this idea with "temperance" of opposing something. Kinesthetic feeling of opposition.
85	chide	1.1	child	I first thot the stimulus word was "child" and then I realized that it was "chide". These words happened to be associated in this way first and then realizing that they were related I reacted with "child".
86	law	.8	book	Visual image of a particular type of law book that I have seen many times lately. The visual image was the basis of the association - I named the object that I saw.
87	virtue	.9	girl	I thot of the last time that I got a word of this sort (See 19). I did not know but that I had been given the word before it so closely fitted in with the atmosphere of some word that was given.
88	reverse	1.3	back	Faint visual image of a lever and the kinesthetic image of pulling it back. The kinesthetic feeling of pulling was very prominent.
89	handsome	.9	good	No visual imagery. Here "good" is an exclamation,- as tho seeing something handsome and saying "good", i.e. "I approve of it".
90	temper	1.2	mad	Visual image of a certain young lady (called up by the preceding stimulus word). She was wandering thru my mind before the stimulus word was given and with the stimulus I saw her turn her back and walk away.
91	heaven	1.0	God	No visual imagery. The idea of "heaven" is always associated with that of "God".
92	quitter	5.4	quit	The association paths were blocked and I kept saying "quitter, quitter, quit...". In saying this it struck me as ridiculous and I started to laugh, thus breaking up the attention to the process of reacting.
93	thrill	.8	delight	Bodily feeling down my spine of a thrill. I think of "thrill" as composed of such sensations as would be aroused by listening to a very fine piece

Observor - II.

No.	Stimulus	Time	Reaction	Introspection
93				of music. "Delight" comes as a description of my feeling. (See 54)
94	character	.7	bad	A little articulatory imagery. "Character" and "bad" have a feeling that is allied,- something common about them. In speaking of character I have a tendency to think of bad character instead of good character.
95	thief	.8	robber	Faint visual image of a brigand with a handkerchief around his head and the feeling of alarm, as if "robber" were an exclamation.
96	guile	1.8	fearless	(Stimulus mistaken for "guide") Some trouble in getting the stimulus. Feeling of moving blindly into things.
97	bully	.7	good	"Bully" and "good" mean exactly the same thing to me.
98	revel	.8	delight	"Delight" did not seem quite right to say. There was the general feeling of exhilaration. (See 93 and 54)
99	revenge	1.5	fight	Very faint visual image of a bucaneer with a sword in his hand. The basis of association was rather that "revenge" means "a fight". Kinesthetic feeling of looking for somebody to oppose.
100	iniquity	.7	bad	The feeling of repulsion which goes with both of these words. (See 94)

Observor - I.

No.	Stimulus	Time	Reaction	Introspection
1	arch	1.5	architecture	Visual image of a particular arch - , "The Marble Arch". My study of architecture deals largely with arches.
2	prude	1.0	girl	I took the word in the French sense.
3	egotism	1.7	altruism	Given as an opposite. I started to react with the French word. French is a language familiar from childhood.
4	single	.8	double	Contrast.
5	chastity	1.6	purity	Synonym. The word chastity brought a visual image of the Illini - I thot of the articles concerning conditions in South America.
6	ginger	5.0	I	(No reaction) "I had it". This referred to the word "sport" which escaped. In England there is a sporting expression "to give ginger", which means to drive a horse hard. I thot of the last Ascott races.
7	shrew	1.2	woman	Thot of the "taming of the shrew". Visual image of the second act of the play.
8	adapt	1.4	admit	The electrical terms "adaptance", "acceptance", "admittance", are all connected.
9	tough	1.0	strong	This again is from engineering experience - tough iron is generally very strong. Visual image of a testing machine.
10	morality	1.5	immorality	Contrast.
11	rubber	1.2	thief	(Stimulus mistaken for "robber") Definition.
12	coquet	3.3	woman	Visual image of a horse. I had a horse called "Koketka".
13	kick	1.0	stop	Visual image of a football. The idea was of the opponents in soccer football stopping the ball.
14	forward	1.2	advance	Visual image of Nansen's ship "Fram", which means "forward". I visited this ship. On a tablet on the deck the name is written in four languages, the one for French being "Avant", which word I thot of.
15	truth	1.0	falshood	These words generally go together - opposites.
16	cake	1.9	butter	Clear visual image of a white "taw cake," with a piece of butter on it, - an English dish, - "muffins".
17	skeptic	1.7	believer	The idea was "unbeliever" and by contrast "believer".

Observor - I.

No.	Stimulus	Time	Reaction	Introspection
18	extort	2.8	drag out	The first idea was "blackmail", but I could not catch the word. The idea was represented by the French "chantager".
19	modest	1.5	proud	Opposite.
20	religion	1.2	unbeliever	Opposite. Visual image of the Unity Club.
21	knife	1.1	fork	Visual image of the Y. M. C. A. restaurant, and particularly the corner table where I ate today.
22	fanatic	1.1	believer	Articulatory. No particular image.
23	insult	1.4	offence	The idea came from having heard recently the talk of Ex-governor Glenn, who spoke about the insult to the white population. He seemed to pronounce the stimulus as tho it were "insu-u-u-lt."
24	flaxen	1.6	white	Clear visual image of a girl whom I know, with white hair - an albino, etc.
25	soul	3.0	Fielding's book	Visual image of the book "The soul of a people". Very generally when I think of a book I see it. Similarly when I think of a quotation I can see it situated on its particular part of the page.
26	bar	1.3	open	The idea was to lift the bar in order to pass . In England, if riding on horse back in the country, one carries a hook and uses it to open the bars. Visual image of a hedge with such a gate.
27	president	1.4	Taft	Articulatory.
28	fluster	3.0	I	(No reaction) "I don't know what that means unless it means to 'rattle'." I don't know why it seemed to have that meaning, but it did.
29	juicy	2.0	power	In the electrical laboratory the current is called "juice".
30	death	1.3	birth	The title of a piece of Russian poetry is "Death is birth". No visual imagery.
31	press	2.0	print	Clear visual image of a printing house, etc.
32	beauty	2.0	rose	The American beauty rose. Visual image of a hotel in London where "American beauties" are sold.
33	retard	1.4	retain	Partly due to the sound and also partly due to the similarity of meaning - thinking of the French "retenir".
34	ghostly	5.7	cemetery	Visual image at once of a cemetery by

Observor - I.

No.	Stimulus	Time	Reaction	Introspection
34				moonlight, but the word did not come. It called up the remembrance of going to the cemetery upon moonlight nights.
35	future	1.1	past	Thot of Ruskin's "Past and future".
36	text	1.3	text book	Visual image of a book with "Text book" printed on it. I could not think what the subject of the book was.
37	success	1.0	failure	Visual image of the "Success" magazine, etc. Articulatory reaction.
38	abstract	1.7	abstract	Visual image of a legal document.
39	fatalism	1.5	pessimism	"Pessimism and fatalism" is the title of an article by a Russian, etc.
40	gauze	4.0	I	(No reaction) "I do not know what that means". This word did not bring up anything, it was entirely meaningless.
41	error	1.6	source	Visual image of an engineering report. At the end of the report is a place for "Sources of error".
42	gargle	1.8	manganese	This is used for a gargle. Visual image of a bottle, etc.
43	energetic	1.4	strong	Visual image of the picture of a man, that appeared on the cover of "System", two or three months ago.
44	apathy	2.0	feeling	Articulatory.
45	silk	1.6	artificial silk	Visual image of a factory which makes artificial silk.
46	stage	1.7	theater	Visual image of the Auditorium.
47	curse	3.3	bless	I had in mind Kipling's poem where a man wishes to curse another, but is afraid to do so, so he says "God bless him", but in such a tone as to be really a curse, etc.
48	duty	1.0	obligation	Articulatory.
49	valor	1.4	power.	Articulatory.
50	velvet	1.1	silk	Visual image of the Liberty Store, London.
51	secure	2.2	tie up	Visual image of a boat.
52	giggle	.8	laugh	Articulatory.
53	inhuman	1.0	cruel	Synonym.
54	ecstacy	2.8	religion	First came the word "church" and then a visual image, etc.
55	lace	5.0	I	(No reaction) "I do not know what it is called in English - "fichut" it is

Observor - I.

No.	Stimulus	Time	Reaction	Introspection
55.				called in French. Visual image of a particular lady wearing a lace fichut, etc.
56	hint	1.3	show	Visual image of a man pointing.
57	blush	1.1	red	Articulatory.
58	wicked	1.0	bad	Synonym. Articulatory.
59	conscience	1.4	money	Thot of "conscience money".
60	shoulder	1.5	arm	I thot of a lecture explaining the action of the shoulder, etc.
61	graft	1.0	money	Articulatory.
62	behave	3.0	comportez vous	Started to react with the French and then hesitated, which lengthened the reaction time.
63	sacrifice	1.8	God	Visual image of a picture in Kipling's book, of Puck's Hill - a picture of a sacrifice, etc.
64	philosophy	.8	science	The two parts of knowledge - "philosophy and science".
65	trifle	1.0	littleness	Used this word with the idea of littleness of character. Thot of the capacity to pay attention to trifles
66	bedlam	1.9	madhood	" Madness " intended. First was the idea of madness and then of Wister's novel "The Virginian"., One of the characters is called "Bedlam".
67	consent	.9	refuse	Logically these words are close together.
68	courage	1.4	fight	Courage can only be shown by a fight. Visual image of a French medal "Pour le courage".
69	cowardice	2.5	fight	At first I did not get the meaning of the word and had to think some time before getting its meaning. Idea and imagery the same as above.(68)
70	course	1.0	running	Visual image of the Illinois field and the running track.
71	habit	1.1	custom	Simply the logical connection.
72	gamble	1.3	play	Visual image of a certain man with whom I have been speaking today. He has just signed a long contract in regard to a fellowship and I asked him if the contract implied that he agree not to drink, not to gamble, etc. The word "play" came probably for two reasons - the idea of playing cards, and also from the French word "jouer".

Observor - I.

No.	Stimulus	Time	Reaction	Introspection
73	purity	1.9	absoluteness	The Buddhist formula is that in order to obtain absolute being one has to preserve purity of mind, of body, etc.
74	drug	1.2	drug store	Visual image of a particular drug store.
75	snake	3.2	serpent	Visual image of a serpent. I had six of them as pets.
76	intention	1.7	hurry	The basis for this I think is Carnegie's saying "Decide and then go fast".
77	caution	1.5	precaution	Visual image of a box of quinine. "Precaution" came from thinking about a situation, represented by this box.
78	alimony	1.3	wife	Visual image of a division of a sheet of the newspaper, with a picture on it etc.
79	atheism	1.7	godlessness	A translation.
80	cuckoo	1.3	a bird	Auditory image of the sound of a cuckoo. Faint visual image of a garden. In my country we have cuckoos in the gardens and for the most part we hear them without seeing them.
81	height	1.3	elevation	Visual image of the class room in hydraulios, the blackboard, etc. We deal with heights and elevations in hydraulics.
82	deject	2.4	throw out	(Stimulus was mistaken for "reject") I thot of the novel "The Irish rebels" which is about the ejection of the Irish peasants.
83	concept	1.9	opposition	What I wished to say, but did not was "antithesis". "Opposition" displaced it. Concept involves synthesis and antithesis.
84	temperance	1.8	dry	Visual image of a situation which occurred yesterday where wet and dry candidates for mayor were discussed. Another image was of the Bedford temperance hotel in London.
85	chide	1.5	abuse	Visual image of the word "chide" spelled out in print. At the very first I thot of "child" and then corrected myself.
86	law	1.6	law school	Visual image of the law building, etc.
87	virtue	7.0	Carnegie's medal	I thot of the Carnegie medal for bravery. The Latin "virtus" meant bravery.
88	reverse	1.1	return	Visual image of an electric double throw switch.
89	handsome	1.1	beautiful	Visual image of an English hansom cab. I then thot that such a reaction

Observor - I.

No.	Stimulus	Time	Reaction	Introspection
89				would be unintelligible in this country and so reacted with "beautiful".
90	temper	1.3	steel	Visual image of tempering steel. I have done a good deal of this lately.
91	heaven	1.4	above	Visual image of the sky.
92	quitter	1.0	man	Visual image of the Saturday Evening Post. Lately a story in it contained a character who repeatedly said "I hate a quitter".
93	thrill	1.7	bird	Recalled the thrilling song of the nightingale. Visual image of how the sounds would be represented in notes.
94	character	1.0	man	Phrase completion. Buffon's expression "Le charactère, c'est l'homme".
95	thief	1.2	robber	Articulatory.
96	guile	1.7	beguile	I understood "guile" to mean "mislead". I thot of "guile" being stronger than "beguile". Both seemed to be connected with the loss of time.
97	bully	1.7	Roosevelt	Roosevelt's own expression.
98	revel	1.7	rebellion	I heard the word correctly, but thot of the Mexican rebels. Visual image of the Mexicans and also of the newspaper headlines.
99	revenge	1.4	vendetta	Thot about my travels in Italy.
100	iniquity	1.2	faithlessness	Thot of a fragment from the Psalms, which is something like this: "Who is worthy of the presence of God and to whom are accessible the heights of Mount Sinai? To the man who has no iniquity in his heart and no faithlessness to his brothers

Observor - J.

No.	Stimulus	Time	Reaction	Introspection
1	arch	1.2	ball	A visual image of the round shape of an arch, which suggested "ball".
2	prude	9.6	I	(No reaction) "I don't know what to say." I did not catch the word at first and was trying to think of the meaning for some time, and felt uneasy when I did not get it. Then vaguely such words as "crude", etc. came into my mind, then I declared "I don't know what to say".
3	egotism	.7	self possession	No visual imagery. Tendency to repeat the stimulus. The connection between "egotism" and "self possession" was a sort of a logical connection since egotistical people seem to be self possessed.
4	single	.7	hard	I do not know how I came to react with this word. It may have been hearing the stop watch click as tho hitting something hard. No visual imagery.
5	chastity	.8	hardness	There seems to be no connection between these.
6	ginger	1.7	bitter	Visual image of ginger, then a gustatory sensation of ginger, which gave a bitter taste.
7	shrew	.8	hard	Visual image of the picture "Taming of the shrew". No connection between this and "hard".
8	adapt	1.4	accommodate	Thot of someone adapting himself to certain circumstances. There was some tendency to repeat the stimulus.
9	tough	.6	hard	Kinesthetic sensation of chewing a tough beef steak. It was hard work.
10	morality	1.3	purity	The idea of morality suggested purity. Tendency to repeat the stimulus.
11	rubber	1.1	tough	Kinesthetic sensation of pulling a rubber, which was hard to do. This led to "tough". "Tough" was a quality of the rubber. Vague visual image of hitting a rubber with a stick and the stick bounding back.
12	coquet	1.5	flirt	Visual image of a coquet. The association seemed very simple.
13	kick	1.2	hit	Vague visual image of someone being kicked and also being hit.
14	forward	1.4	agriculturist	(Mistook the stimulus for "farmer") Visual image of a farmer, etc.
15	truth	.6	hard	Seemed to think of a synonym for truth, but before I could say it "hard" came out.
16	cake	.7	pie	Visual image of a cake and then of a table with both cake and pie on it.

Observor - J.

No.	Stimulus	Time	Reaction	Introspection
17	skeptic	4.7	doubter	I inhibited "hard". I thot of a synonym for skeptic.
18	extort	1.3	hurt	Visual image of someone trying to make a child say something. The person was hurting the child because he would not say it.
19	modest	1.9	bluff	I again inhibited "hard". I do not know how I got "bluff". Vague visual image of a modest person.
20	religion	1.2	sin	Visual image of a church. This faded rapidly and then I thot of what religion was for, which suggested "sin"
21	knife	1.2	fork	Visual image of the same dinner table as mentioned before (See 16) with a knife and fork, etc. on it.
22	fanatic	1.5	heretic	Visual image of a fanatical person of the time of the middle ages. This same person seemed to be a heretic.
23	insult	1.7	blame	Visual image of the word "insult" written out. A second visual image of someone insulting another person, and the second person was to blame for it.
24	flaxen	1.2	white	Visual image of a light haired girl. There was a tendency to say "red", but it did not come.
25	soul	1.0	body	I have just been studying in philosophy the relation between the soul and the body. Faint visual image of the two words heading a paragraph.
26	bar	1.2	growl	(Stimulus mistaken for "bark") Visual image of a dog and I also heard him bark.
27	president	1.9	general	Vague visual image of someone who was the president of the United States. The fact of the president being commander in chief of the army led to "general". I thot of Grant.
28	fluster	1.0	blur	Visual image of it snowing, making a blur on the window pane.
29	juicy	.8	white	Visual image of a juicy white peach.
30	death	1.9	alive	Faint visual image of a dead person.
31	press	1.2	push	Visual image of a man having something between two boards and pressing down.
32	beauty	1.3	clean	Visual image of things perfectly clean and white. There was a tendency to say white.
33	retard	1.3	push	I imagined myself in a push ball contest trying to keep someone from getting past me. Visual and kinesthetic, mostly visual.

Observor - J.

No.	Stimulus	Time	Reaction	Introspection
34	ghostly	1.4	white	Visual image of someone dressed up in a white sheet, etc.
35	future	.9	near	I thot of the future and that the present time, or time near at hand, was the opposite of future time.
36	text	.8	book	Visual image of a text book.
37	success	.9	failure	Visual image of a particular man who has been successful in business.
38	abstract	.7	concrete	The two words have always been associated in my mind. Faint visual image of one word written after the other.
39	fatalism	1.3	beauty	I thot of some man being killed. I could see it as tho it were in a dungeon. I probably thot of the word "beauty" because of the phrase "curses on thy fatal beauty". I did not think of this phrase definitely before reacting.
40	gauze	1.3	white	Visual image of the gauze used in bandaging and the doctor unrolling some. It was white. There was a tendency to say "thin".
41	error	1.0	mistake	Synonym. No imagery.
42	gargle	1.8	gurgle	Visual image of myself gargling and I could feel it bubbling up in my throat.
43	energetic	1.0	brave	Visual image of a soldier of mediaeval times.
44	apathy	1.6	contempt	Thot of something that was disgusting. The word "apathy" has that meaning for me. The reaction seemed to be synonymous with the stimulus.
45	silk	.7	satin	Visual image of a piece of silk. The words "silk" and "satin" are associated in my mind.
46	stage	1.2	vaudeville	Visual image of the Orpheum, particularly the stage.
47	curse	1.1	swear	Synonyms. No imagery.
48	duty	1.1	plain	The phrase "plain duty" occurred to me.
49	valor	.7	bravery	Visual image of a soldier of the early times, etc. He was defending a pass. A story about the Greeks came to my mind. (See,43)
50	velvet	.7	soft	Visual image of velvet and then I felt it. Cutaneous image of it.
51	secure	.8	safe	Visual image of a house that was locked up and of myself being inside of it and thus being safe.
52	giggle	.7	laugh	Visual image of a little girl, etc. giggling. No auditory imagery.

Observor - J.

No.	Stimulus	Time	Reaction	Introspection
53	inhuman	1.7	safe	There were a number of words that came into my mind. One was "barbarous." Thot of a condition where there was no inhumanity and that such conditions would be safe. (See 51)
54	ecstacy	1.1	joy	Very indistinct visual image of a bunch of people in a grove having lots of fun.
55	lace	1.7	rent	(Mistook the stimulus for "lease") Vague visual image of a house and the idea of renting it.
56	hint	2.4	suggestion	Inhibited the word "plain". Tried to think of a synonym.
57	blush	.8	red	Visual image of a person blushing.
58	wicked	.9	sin	Synonym.
59	conscience	.9	hurt	Thot of the phrase "his conscience hurt him".
60	shoulder	1.3	blade	Thot of the phrase "shoulder blade". Faint visual imagery of a bone.
61	graft	2.0	money	I thot of the object of graft.
62	behave	2.0	sin	Visual image of a young man running around hitting people and not doing just as he should.
63	sacrifice	1.3	pain	Visual image of an animal being sacrificed on the alter and the animal showed that he was suffering pain.
64	philosophy	4.1	fool	I thot of a course in philosophy, but there was nothing that came to my mind to say. Then I thot of the opposite of philosophers.
65	trifle	1.8	page	Visual image of a page in the court of a queen. A mediaeval picture again. The page was not very conscientious about his duty.
66	bedlam	1.8	confusion	Visual image of a lot of people running around, etc.
67	consent	1.3	give	Thot of the phrase "give consent".
68	courage	1.0	bravery	Very vague visual imagery. "Bravery" thot of as a synonym.
69	cowardice	1.3	bravery	"Bravery", the opposite of "cowardice," came very easily. (See 68)
70	course	1.0	rough	(Stimulus taken as "coarse") Visual image of a coarse piece of cloth and it felt rough between my fingers.
71	habit	1.1	content	Visual image of a man sitting beside his fireside and he was contented.
72	gamble	1.7	drink	Visual image of a gambler leaning up against a bar in a saloon.
73	purity	1.0	chastity	Synonym.

Observor - J.

No.	Stimulus	Time	Reaction	Introspection
74	drug	1.4	swing	(Stimulus mistaken for "drunk") Visual image of a drunkard walking down the street and swinging from side to side.
75	snake	1.1	crawl	Visual image of a snake crawling along the grass. Little organic feeling of repulsion.
76	intention	2.1	intend	A tendency to repeat the stimulus. Thot that a person who has an intention intends to do something.
77	caution	1.9	pain	Visual image of a man who, having been cautioned not to pick up something, did it and it hurt him.
78	alimony	1.4	marry	Went back from alimony to divorce and then to marriage.
79	atheism	2.0	God	Thot of the opposite of atheism.
80	cuckoo	.8	bird	Visual image of a clock and a cuckoo bird coming out, etc.
81	height	2.1	stiff	(Stimulus taken as "white") Kinesthetic sensation of having a stiff white shirt on, etc.
82	deject	1.2	turn down	I seemed to hear "reject". After I had reacted I knew the stimulus had been "deject". Vis. im. of a man turned down.
83	concept	1.9	idea	The two words "concept" and "idea" seemed to go together.
84	temperance	1.5	drink	The idea of temperance and its opposite.
85	chide	1.9	bid	The idea that came was that of bidding a man to be good. Vague visual image of a child which someone was chastising.
86	law	1.0	order	The phrase "law and order" came.
87	virtue	.9	bravery	Visual image of a knight and thot of the knightly virtues.
88	reverse	1.4	apply	The idea was that of applying the reverse to an engine. Visual image of a reverse lever and also slight kinesthetic imagery.
89	handsome	1.7	beautiful	Visual image of a handsome man.
90	temper	2.0	abstain	(Stimulus mistaken for temperate) The idea of temperate was that of some one abstaining.
91	heaven	.9	earth	Visual image of both the earth and sky.
92	quitter	3.5	abstainer	The idea was that of a man in the foot-ball field who was a quitter, but I could not think of any word that would suit him. Finally thot of abstaining from getting into the game. Immediately following was

Observor - J.

No.	Stimulus	Time	Reaction	Introspection
92				the idea of "yellow".
93	thrill	1.1	please	Visual image of a show and a thrilling pleasant scene.
94	character	1.3	play	The idea of a show was still in my mind. I thot of a character play. No visual imagery.
95	thief	1.0	robber	Visual image of a man climbing a porch, etc.
96	guile	2.0	song	Stimulus mistaken for "Guild") I thot of Professor Guild and the song he has written. Visual image of both Professor Guild and the cover of "Illinois Loyalty".
97	bully	.9	brave	Visual image of an Indian brave bullying some victim that he had.
98	revel	1.4	debauch	Visual image of a scene of revelry, etc.
99	revenge	2.5	contrast	The idea of a man taking revenge and of a man who would not do so. Then the idea of contrast between them.
100	iniquity	1.0	sin	Synonym.

Observor - K.

No.	Stimulus	Time	Reaction	Introspection
1	arch	1.4	curve	Visual image of a stone arch, etc.
2	prude	1.2	problem	(Stimulus mistaken for "problem") Visual image of a problem on the blackboard.
3	egotism	1.3	man	Auditory image of someone speaking of another person as being egotistical. Also visual image of a man.
4	single	1.1	horse	Visual image of a single horse hitched to a rig. I also had an auditory image of the horse travelling.
5	chastity	3.2	dictionary	At first I did not quite understand the word. I had a visual image of myself looking it up in a dictionary, probably also slight kinesthetic image of looking it up.
6	ginger	.7	bread	Phrase completion idea. Visual image of ginger bread - this came before reaction.
7	shrew	2.7	taming of the shrew	Visual image of an advertisement of "The taming of the shrew".
8	adapt	1.1	mathematics	Faint visual image of the word "mathematics". The idea was that of being "adapt" ("apt" probably in mind) at mathematics.
9	tough	1.0	meat	Visual and kinesthetic imagery of tough meat. Possible a little of the phrase completion idea.
10	morality	1.0	church	Visual image of a church.
11	rubber	1.0	tree	Phrase completion idea and visual image of a tree.
12	coquet	1.0	girl	Visual image.
13	kick	1.0	rope	(Stimulus mistaken for "kink") Visual image of a rope with a kink in it.
14	forward	.8	man	I said "man", tho I was thinking of a young boy - a forward fellow. Visual imagery.
15	truth	1.3	girl	Visual image of a girl. This may be the result of a conversation the other day concerning the truthfulness of some girls.
16	cake	1.4	girl	(Mistook the stimulus for "Kate") Visual image of a girl in general, then it became a particular pretty girl whose name is "Kate".
17	skeptic	1.1	man	Visual and auditory image of a man in general. I did not hear any particular words, but just the idea of hearing him speak.
18	extort	1.2	punishment	Visual image representing the extortion of evidence by inflicting punishment.

Observor - K.

No.	Stimulus	Time	Reaction	Introspection
19	modest	1.3	man	This should have been rather "mankind", than "man". Vague visual imagery, etc.
20	religion	.7	church	Visual image of the interior of a church. (See 10)
21	knife	.7	cut	Visual image of cutting my finger with a knife and then the organic sensation of drawing back.
22	fanatic	1.3	man	Visual image of a man lecturing. He seemed to be a fanatic lecturing on some hobby. All except the visual image is very indistinct.
23	insult	1.4	man	Visual image of a person insulting another in a quarrel. The actions of the insulted person were prominent.
24	flaxen	1.7	wool	Visual image of flax. The word "wool" was not the one I wanted. I wanted something to represent this visual image of flax. "Wool" came because of its being in shreds, something like flax.
25	soul	2.6	philosophy	Visual image of a class room in philosophy and a discussion, etc.
26	bar	1.2	fence	Visual image of a fence with a bar across, etc.
27	president	2.6	United States	First a visual image of Washington, the White House , etc. The name "United States" seemed to represent this entire group.
28	fluster	1.4	person	Visual image of a person talking and being embarrassed.
29	juicy	.8	orange	Visual image of an orange and then the kinesthetic sensation of eating it. Also olfactory sensation and possibly faint cutaneous sensation.
30	death	.9	person	Visual image of a funeral. First it was a funeral in general and later a specific one.
31	press	1.7	newspaper	Visual image of seeing a newspaper being printed. There was a tendency as I was reacting to say "newspaper agent".
32	beauty	.9	girl	Visual image of a pretty girl.
33	retard	.6	bed	(Stimulus mistaken for "retire") Visual image of seeing myself going to bed - I being away from myself.
34	ghostly	1.2	death	Visual image of a ghost - a figure completely shrouded in white and having a very dark face. I could not see thru it, except the head. The face was like a black skull.

Observor - K.

No.	Stimulus	Time	Reaction	Introspection
35	future	1.3	person	No visual imagery. I thot of something coming in the future. This idea was in connection with human beings.
36	text	.6	book	First a visual image and then phrase completion idea.
37	success	.8	man	Visual image of a business man.
38	abstract	1.3	law	Thot of abstracting a case. No visual imagery.
39	fatalism	2.4	philosophy	Visual image, seeing myself reading about fatalism. The "ism" as much as anything else led to the reaction.
40	gauze	1.0	cloth	Visual image of physician's gauze.
41	error	1.2	arithmetic	Visual image of an error in a problem.
42	gargle	.9	throat	Kinesthetic feeling of gargling. Also visual image of myself gargling.
43	energetic	.6	man	Visual image of a man working hard at manual labor.
44	apathy	2.7	dictionary	Visual image that took me back to the word "chastity" (5). Same imagery as in that case. First I had a visual image of myself as I was when the word "chastity" was given.
45	silk	.5	cloth	Visual image of silk cloth.
46	stage	2.8	theater	Visual image of the stage of a theater. There was a conflict between "opera" and "theater".
47	curse	1.0	man	I do not know how this reaction came about. No visual imagery.
48	duty	2.8	army	Visual image of a soldier performing sentinel duty.
49	valor	1.4	gallant	Visual image of the knights of olden times and their gallantry and valor.
50	velvet	.8	cloth	Visual imagery.
51	secure	1.0	padlock	Visual image of a shed with a padlock on the door.
52	giggle	.7	girl	Visual image of a girl laughing hysterically.
53	inhuman	1.2	animal	There was a sort of an opposite feeling. Visual image of an animal, and then I thot of something just the opposite.
54	ecstacy	1.0	person	Visual image of a boy who was joyous about something.
55	lace	1.2	cloth	Visual image of a piece of lace, etc.
56	hint	1.7	exam	Visual image of a professor giving a little talk before the examination questions were given. I thot of

Observor - K.

No.	Stimulus	Time	Reaction	Introspection
56				him as giving a hint.
57	blush	.8	girl	Visual image of a girl blushing.
58	wicked	.8	man	Visual image of a villain in a play.
59	conscience	.8	man	I thot of a man as having a conscience. Articulatory. Later a visual image of a man.
60	shoulder	1.9	gun	Visual image of a soldier carrying a gun over his shoulder. I thot of "gun" some time before I said it. There was a conflict between "gun" and "soldier" which caused the hesitation.
61	graft	1.2	corporation	Articulatory. Then visual image of a trustees room and meeting.
62	behave	.7	boy	Visual image of a mother telling her little boy to behave.
63	sacrifice	.9	person	Visual image of a person sacrificing some pleasure for the happiness of someone else. The indication of sacrifice is hardly visual - rather an idea.
64	philosophy	1.0	book	Visual image of a philosophy book.
65	trifle	1.9	mere matter	Articulatory.
66	bedlam	1.6	humdrum	Auditory image of a noise and then a visual image of a great commotion. This seemed to be continual and of a humdrum monotony.
67	consent	1.0	person	Visual image of a person receiving the consent of someone else to do something. I was at a distance and knew that he was getting the consent of the other person.
68	courage	.7	person	Visual image of a person in general. This person became a soldier.
69	cowardice	1.2	same	("Same" was given to indicate "person") Visual image of a retired soldier.
70	course	.9	cloth	Visual image of burlap.
71	habit	1.2	person	Articulatory.
72	gamble	1.0	man	Visual image of a gambling den, with people, etc.
73	purity	1.0	maiden	Articulatory. Connected this with a book or story.
74	drug	.7	drug store	Visual image of a drug store, etc. Phrase completion idea probably shortened the time.
75	snake	1.3	snake	Visual image of a snake.

Observor - K.

No.	Stimulus	Time	Reaction	Introspection
76	intention	.7	man	Articulatory. The idea of a man having the intention of doing something.
77	caution	.9	person	First was the idea of a person in general and immediately following it was the visual image of a mother cautioning her child.
78	alimony	2.0	drug	"Alimony" brought the word "sal ammoniac" and then I thot of a drug store in visual terms. I was fully aware that the stimulus was "alimony".
79	atheism	1.2	atheist	Sound reaction. I did not think of the meaning until after reaction.
80	cuckoo	.7	bird	Visual image of a bird, followed by an auditory image.
81	height	1.0	mountain	Visual image of a high mountain peak.
82	deject	.8	person	Visual image of a gloomy person.
83	concept	1.1	man	Visual image of a fellow in a psychology class discussing concepts with the professor. The idea of this fellow led to the reaction.
84	temperance	1.3	man	Visual image of a man lecturing on temperance.
85	chide	1.9	boy	Visual image of a mother chiding her boy.
86	law	1.0	law building	Visual image of the law building.
87	virtue	.8	girl	Articulatory.
88	reverse	1.0	automobile	Visual image of going backwards in an automobile. Also kinesthetic imagery of throwing the levers.
89	handsome	1.0	girl	Visual image of a girl. "Man" would seem to be a more appropriate reaction.
90	temper	1.0	man	Visual image of a man in a rage.
91	heaven	.6	sky	Visual image of the sky. There was connected with it the idea of vastness and great height.
92	quitter	1.3	boy	Articulatory at first. Then a visual image of a bunch of young fellows calling another a quitter.
93	thrill	1.4	man	Kinesthetic feeling of a thrill running thru me. Articulatory.
94	character	1.1	person	I thot of a person having character. The phrase "personal character" came. Phrase completion, inverted.
95	thief	.6	man	I thot first of men in general as being thieves. Then a visual image of a man in the act of robbing. Articulatory reaction.

Observor - K.

No.	Stimulus	Time	Reaction	Introspection
96	guile	3.4	gild	Sound reaction. No imagery or meaning. At first confused and thot of lots of things, all of them conflicting.
97	bully	.7	boy	Visual image of a bully.
98	revel	1.0	revelation	Word completion reaction.
99	revenge	1.0	man	I had the idea of man taking revenge . Articulatory.
100	iniquity	3.9	bible	First a confusion. I thot of various connections, particularly of where and in what connection I had heard the word. Each of the conflicting ideas seemed separate and I finally decided on one of them - "bible".

Observor - L.

No.	Stimulus	Time	Reaction	Introspection
1	arch	1.7	masonry	Visual image of an arch of masonry.
2	prude	1.9	problem	(Mistook the stimulus for "prove"). Thot of a problem in arithmetic.
3	egotism	2.4	I	Visual image of a capital "I".
4	single	1.2	married	Opposite.
5	chastity	1.3	obedience	Visual image of a monk taking the oath of "poverty, chastity and obedience". Phrase completion idea.
6	ginger	1.9	ginger bread	Visual image of a cake of ginger bread.
7	shrew	1.7	Shakespere	Visual image of the title "Taming of the shrew", etc.
8	adapt	1.6	adaptability	Word completion. The meaning of the stimulus word was clear.
9	tough	2.4	meat	Visual image of a tough piece of meat. In kinesthetic imagery I tried to cut it and felt disappointed at not being able to.
10	morality	2.0	church	Reaction articulatory. Visual image of a church. I repeated the stimulus. In many of these the stimulus is repeated before association.
11	rubber	.9	boot	Visual image of a pair of boots I used to possess.
12	coquet	1.0	girl	Visual image of a coquet, in general.
13	kick	.8	horse	Visual image of a horse,- the horse was not kicking.
14	forward	.9	march	Phrase completion.
15	truth	2.5	veracity	Articulatory. There was a little hesitation at first and a search for a word.
16	cake	1.2	knife	Visual image of a cake on a plate with a knife beside it.
17	skeptic	1.7	Hindoos	I was going to say "hypocrite". Visual image of an old bent over man with a cane. Sound association between "hypocrite" and "Hindoos".
18	extort	1.2	extortionist	Visual image of a contortionist, etc. I got mixed up on the words in reacting.
19	modest	4.2	modest	Thot of an exemplary young maiden, etc. in visual imagery. The word I was going to react with was "prude."
20	religion	1.3	church	Articulatory. Visual image of a church probably not until after the reaction.
21	knife	1.3	cut	Visual image of a cut in my finger.
22	fanatic	1.9	religion	Articulatory. The ideawas that there

Observor - L.

No.	Stimulus	Time	Reaction	Introspection
22				are many religious fanatics.
23	insult	1.7	slam	Articulatory. Synonym.
24	flaxen	1.0	hair	Visual image of a flaxen haired girl.
25	soul	1.7	heart	Articulatory.
26	bar	1.4	Tennyson	I have on the wall in my room a little piece of poetry by Tennyson "Crossing the Bar".
27	president	1.6	Roosevelt	Visual image of Roosevelt, on horseback, etc.
28	fluster	13.3	woman	Visual image of a woman in a fluster. I was not real sure of the stimulus word at first and then thot that I would try to associate something anyway, taking the word as fluster.
29	juicy	1.5	orange	Visual image of an orange. My mouth watered slightly.
30	death	1.0	grave	Visual image of an open grave, with people gathered around, etc.
31	press	1.1	paper	Visual image of a printing press, etc.
32	beauty	1.7	rose	The American beauty is the kind I thot of.
33	retard	2.7	bed	(Stimulus mistaken for "retire") Visual image of my bed. At first there was a little hesitancy because I was not sure of the stimulus.
34	ghostly	1.3	Poe	I have been reading his tales. Articulatory.
35	future	1.9	fortune teller	Visual image of a Gipsy woman in a tent, etc. Visual image of the sign in front which said "She reads your future".
36	text	1.0	preacher	Visual image of a preacher in a pulpit preaching from the text.
37	success	1.9	magazine	Visual image of the Success magazine.
38	abstract	1.2	statement	Associated the words "abstract statement". Articulatory.
39	fatalism	1.5	Mohammed	Articulatory.
40	gauze	1.1	underwear	Articulatory.
41	error	1.6	mistake	Articulatory.
42	gargle	1.3	medicine	Visual image of a bottle of medicine, etc.
43	energetic	1.5	business-like	Articulatory. Faint visual image of a man.

Observor - L.

No.	Stimulus	Time	Reaction	Introspection
44	apathy	1.9	sickness	Articulatory. Very doubtful of the meaning of the word.
45	silk	1.3	store	Visual image of a certain store with silk on the shelves.
46	stage	2.0	theater	Visual image of the Walker.
47	curse	2.0	man	Visual image of a man cursing a dog - a remembrance of a particular instance.
48	duty	1.6	joy	Articulatory. The idea was that what is one's duty should be their joy.
49	valor	1.4	bravery	Articulatory.
50	velvet	1.3	store	Visual image of some velvet cloaks in a particular store.
51	secure	1.2	safe	Thot of the phrase "safe and sound".
52	giggle	1.0	laugh	Visual image of a girl giggling.
53	inhuman	1.9	brute	Visual image of a man beating a horse.
54	ecstacy	1.3	joy	Articulatory.
55	lace	1.5	skirt	Visual image of a girl with a white dress and lace around the bottom.
56	hint	3.0	hunch	Articulatory. Hesitation in reaction on account of the slang nature of the reaction word.
57	blush	1.4	apple	Visual image of an apple with a blush on its cheek.
58	wicked	1.7	sinful	Articulatory..
59	conscience	1.7	soul	Articulatory.
60	shoulder	3.0	right	Thot of the expression "right shoulder arms". Visual image of the cadets. Phrase completion, inverted.
61	graft	2.1	stockholder	Faint visual image of a bloated stockholder - a grafter.
62	behave	1.7	school boy	Visual image of a teacher reprimanding a young boy, etc.
63	sacrifice	1.8	crucifixion	Visual image of Christ on the cross.
64	philosophy	2.4	Bode	Visual image of Professor Bode instructing one of his classes.
65	trifle	1.7	trifling	"Trifle" was thot of as a noun and "trifling" as a verb.
66	bedlam	1.6	confusion	Articulatory.
67	consent	1.6	proposal	Visual image of a picture that appeared in Life, etc.
68	courage	2.1	bravery	Visual image of an army officer, etc.

Observor - L.

No.	Stimulus	Time	Reaction	Introspection
69	cowardice	3.3	sneak	Visual image of a man sneaking away in the dark from something that he had done.
70	course	2.6	Literature and Arts	Phrase completion. I am taking the Literature and Arts course.
71	habit	1.3	smoking	Visual image of a particular man, who is addicted to the cigaret habit, smoking.
72	gamble	1.2	cards	Articulatory.
73	purity	3.7	statue	Visual image of the statue of Justice, situated in my home town and which I passed on the way to school, blindfolded and holding up the scales. I have always had the conception of perfect justice, purity, etc. belonging to this statue.
74	drug	1.7	store	Visual image of a drug store, etc.- a particular drug store.
75	snake	1.1	woods	Visual image of a snake crawling around in the leaves. Also a slight shuddering feeling of getting away as fast as possible.
76	intention	2.3	good	Phrase completion, inverted.
77	caution	2.5	automobile	Visual image of a man whom I saw last Sunday driving an automobile very cautiously - the first one I have ever seen.
78	alimony	1.3	divorce	Articulatory.
79	atheism	2.7	pantheism	Articulatory. Likely the "ism" found in both words led to the result.
80	cuckoo	1.3	bird	Visual image of a particular cuckoo clock with the bird coming out, etc. The image came after the reaction word.
81	height	2.4	steep	Visual image of a particular hill, etc.
82	deject	1.2	reject	Sound reaction.
83	concept	1.4	conception	Word completion.
84	temperance	1.5	W.C.T.U.	Visual image of the fountain in front of the Flat Iron building, given by the W. C. T. U.
85	chide	1.8	scorn	Articulatory. Thot of a person chiding another and that it was done in a scornful way.
86	law	1.4	order	Completion of the phrase "law and order".
87	virtue	1.8	praise	Thot of the passage in the Bible "If there be any virtue, if there be any praise ...".

Observor - L.

No.	Stimulus	Time	Reaction	Introspection
88	reverse	1.2	engine	Visual image of an engineer throwing on the reverse lever.
89	handsome	2.1	cab	(Stimulus mistaken for "hansom") Visual image of a hansom cab.
90	temper	1.8	temperance	Word completion.
91	heaven	1.1	hell	Thot of "Heaven or hell".
92	quitter	2.2	cow	(Stimulus mistaken for "critter") One often hears an old man speak of a cow as a "critter".
93	thrill	3.0	chill	Sound reaction.
94	character	2.3	building	Visual image of a wall representing character, in which were stones representing truth, honesty, etc. The idea of this wall led to "building".
95	thief	1.0	robber	Visual image of a robber, etc.
96	guile	3.0	play	(Stimulus mistaken for "Guild") I thot of Professor Guild - the man who coaches plays.
97	bully	1.3	boy	Visual image of a certain boy - a bully-whom I knew as a youngster.
98	revel	1.3	reveille	Word completion. Faint visual image of a trumpeter.
99	revenge	2.0	avenge	Sound reaction.
100	iniquity	1.4	evil	Articulatory.

Observor - A.

SUMMARY.

Consecutive or simultaneous ideas				Type of situation recalled					Accompanying imagery					
				Particular		General								
Wd.	Time			Visual	Other		Visual	Other	Au.	Vi.	Ki.	Cl.	2d	Nn
1	1.8	56	2.0	2	4		5	1	4	2	2	Gu.	Ar.	1
2	2.2	57	1.4	11	12		7	3	10	3	3	Gu.	11	6
3	2.0	58	1.0	16	36		8	6	11	5	23	Au.	12	2
4	1.2	59	1.2	27	42		9	17	12	8	31	44	16	
5	.6	60	1.3	32	45		10	23	19	9	42	G	17	
6	1.4	61	1.2	48	47		13	31	22	10	59	50	30	
7	1.0	62	1.8	64	78		14	33	29	11	6	Cu	34	
8	1.0	63	2.0	66	7		15	52	32	13			41	
9	1.2	64	1.8	69			18	59	35	14		2	44	
10	1.4	65	1.3	81			19	62	36	15			47	
11	1.0	66	1.2	87			20	65	42	16			52	
12	1.0	67	1.8	95			21	74	45	18			59	
13	1.4	68	1.6	97			22	80	55	19			70	
14	1.4	69	1.6	13			24	92	56	20			80	
15	1.8	70	2.0				25	96	62	21			96	
16	1.4	71	2.0				26	98	63	22			97	
17	1.0	72	2.0				28	38	65	24			100	
18	1.8	73	.8				29	17	67	25			16	
19	1.4	74	1.3				30		68	26				
20	1.0	75	1.1				34		71	27				
21	1.0	76	1.6				35		74	28				
22	2.2	77	1.2				36		75	29				
23	1.4	78	2.0				40		76	30				
24	1.6	79	2.4				43		78	32	Vi.			
25	1.4	80	1.4				44		83	33				
26	2.0	81	1.4				46		86	34	76			
27	2.0	82	1.2				50		92	35	77			
28	2.0	83	2.0				51		94	36	79			
29	1.2	84	2.0				54		98	39	81			
30	1.8	85	1.4				55		99	40	82			
31	2.2	86	1.0				53		38	41	83			
32	1.2	87	1.6				49		31	43	84			
33	1.8	88	1.2				41			44	85			
34	1.1	89	1.4				39			46	86		2d	
35	3.6	90	2.2				56			49	88		Vi.	
36	1.2	91	1.2				57			50	89		48	
37	1.6	92	1.6				58			51	90		69	
38	2.0	93	1.2			Vis.	60			53	91		87	
39	1.0	94	.8			88	61			54	93		3	
40	1.3	95	1.2			89	63			55	94			
41	1.3	96	1.2			90	67			56	95			
42	1.2	97	1.2			91	68			57	99			
43	1.0	98	2.2			93	70			58	100			
44	1.0	99	2.0			94	71			60	74			
45	1.1	100	1.8			99	72			61				
46	1.4					100	73			63				
47	1.2	1Q	1.2			63	75			64				
48	1.4	2Q	1.4				76			66				
49	1.0	3Q	1.8				77			67				
50	1.2						79			68				
51	1.2						82			70				
52	1.6						83			71				
53	1.0						84			72				
54	1.6						85			73				
55	1.2						86			75				

Observor - A.

SUMMARY.

Sound & syn. change	Word, phrase & idea comp.	Identity	Contrast	CO-existence	Predicate	Judgment of quality	Subordination
42	4	11	14	2	1	30	8
45	29	18	38	37	5	34	15
52	36	22	2	46	7	44	20
85	71	26		57	9	78	39
4	74	31		62	12	98	48
	75	32		64	13	5	53
	76	33		67	16		58
	86	40		68	17		70
	94	43		84	19		8
		49		93	24		
	9	50		89	25		
		51		11	27		
		56			41 31		
		65			54		
		66			55		
		77			60		
		81			61		
		82			63		
		88			69		
		92			72		
		97			73		
		21			79		
					80		
					83		
					87		
					89		
					90		
					91		
					95		
					96		
					100		
					36		

Coordination	Supraordination	Egocentric	Ego. predicate	Subject relation	Object relation	Causality	Failure
6		3		21			
10		23					
28		47					
35		59					
4		4					

Observor - B. SUMMARY.

Consecutive or simultaneous ideas				Type of situation recalled: Particular		General		Accompanying imagery					
Wd.	Time			Visual	Other	Visual	Other	Au.	Vi.	Ki.	Cl.	2d	Nn
1	1.2	56	3.0	3	2	6	11	7	1	11	Gu.	Ar.	4
2	1.2	57	1.0	12	4	11	5	8	2	13	Cu.	4	10
3	1.3	58	.8	18	8	13	7	9	3	48	Au.	14	2
4	.8	59	1.0	22	10	14	9	14	5	50	6	70	
5	2.5	60	2.2	31	23	15	17	15	6	99	Cu.	73	
6	1.2	61	2.0	32	25	16	20	17	8	5	50	76	
7	1.3	62	1.0	37	27	19	38	20	11		Cu.	77	
8	3.0	63	2.0	42	33	21	48	22	12		2	6	
9	1.3	64	1.0	43	34	24	68	23	13				
10	1.1	65	2.0	44	35	26	78	25	14				
11	1.1	66	1.3	51	36	28	79	26	15				
12	.9	67	1.3	58	41	29	80	27	16				
13	.6	68	3.0	59	46	3o	81	33	18				
14	1.1	69	1.2	61	47	39	85	35	19				
15	1.1	70	.8	71	65	40	87	36	20				
16	1.7	71	1.7	82	66	45	99	38	21				
17	1.0	72	1.0	83	70	49	16	39	22				
18	.7	73	1.0	84	76	50		41	24				
19	1.0	74	.8	86	77	52		42	25				
20	1.0	75	.9	88	92	53		47	26				
21	.8	76	2.0	96	93	54		52	28				
22	1.1	77	1.7	21	95	55		65	29				
23	1.0	78	1.0		22	56		66	30				
24	.9	79	.9			57		68	31				
25	1.2	80	.9			60		78	32				
26	2.2	81	.9			62		79	35				
27	1.4	82	1.0			63		80	39				
28	1.0	83	1.3			64		81	40				
29	.7	84	1.3			67		82	42				
30	.9	85	1.0			69		83	45				
31	1.0	86	1.0			72		84	46	Vi			
32	1.3	87	1.0			73		85	47	83			
33	.8	88	2.1			74		87	48	84			
34	.8	89	.8			75		88	49	86		2d	
35	.5	90	1.6			89		91	50	87		Vi.	
36	1.0	91	.8			90		92	51	88		34	
37	1.0	92	1.0			91		93	52	90		37	
38	1.0	93	1.1			94		94	53	91		43	
39	3.4	94	1.9			97		95	54	92		44	
40	1.2	95	.6			98		96	55	93		58	
41	1.1	96	5.0			100		97	56	94		59	
42	1.0	97	1.0			41		98	57	95		61	
43	1.0	98	1.3					99	60	96		7	
44	.8	99	1.0					100	62	97			
45	1.0	100	.9					44	63	98			
46	.8	1Q	.9						67	100			
47	.8	2Q	1.0						69	70			
48	.9	3Q	1.3						71				
49	.9								72				
50	1.2	1Q=1st							73				
51	.5	quartile.							74				
52	1.3	etc.							75				
53	.7								76				
54	1.0								77				
55	1.0								82				

Observor - B. SUMMARY.

Sound & syn. change	Word, phrase & idea comp.	Identi-ty	Contrast	CO-existence	Predi-cate	Judg-ment of quality	Sobor-dina-tion
65	4	8	30	23	1	13	20
96	9	92	38	25	5	31	18
2	26	93	87	33	6	45	17
	27	100	3	34	10	72	39
	29	4		35	11	85	70
	36			37	14	5	5
	41			42	16		
	46			63	19		
	74			64	24		
	80			67	28		
	86			75	32		
	91			78	40		
	95			79	43		
	98			83	44		
	14			14	47		
					48		
					49		
					50		
					51		
					52		
					53		
					54		
					55		
					57		
					58		
					60		
					61		
					62		
					66	Pred.	
					69	90	
					73	97	
					76	38	
					82	--	
					84	43	
					88		
					89		

Coordi-nation	Supra-ordina-tion	Egocen-tric	Ego.pre-dicate	Subject relation	Object rela-tion	Causal-ity	Failure
15	2			21	77	99	
56	3						
86	7						
71	12						
81	22						
94	59						
6	6						

Observor - C.

SUMMARY.

Consecutive or simultaneous ideas: Wd:	Ide-Time	:	:	Type of situation recalled: Particular: Visual	Particular: Other	General: Visual	General: Other	Accompanying Imagery: Ar.	Vi.	Ki.	Ol.	2d	Nn
1	2.0	56	6.2	12	9	2	3	1	2	35	Gu.	Ar.	
2	1.6	57	.9	55	28	13	4	3	12	42	Cu.	50	
3	4.4	58	.8	2	66	21	5	4	13		Au.	93	
4	1.4	59	1.3		91	34	6	5	21	2	6	94	
5	1.1	60	.6		4	4	7	7	34		Cu.	3	
6	1.3	61	1.4				8	9	13		16		
7	1.8	62	.7				10	10	5		Gu.		
8	2.8	63	3.6				11	11			29		
9	1.4	64	.6				14	14			Cu.		
10	8.0	65	4.1			Other	15	15			45		
11	1.1	66	.9			64	16	17			Cu.		
12	4.4	67	1.7			65	17	18			50		
13	2.0	68	1.1			67	18	19			Cu.		
14	1.1	69	1.8			68	19	20			5		
15	2.3	70	1.0			69	20	22					
16	1.4	71	2.0			70	22	23			L		
17	2.5	72	1.2			71	23	24					
18	1.7	73	2.0			72	24	25	Ar.				
19	1.4	74	1.3			73	25	26	69				
20	4.0	75	1.7			74	26	27	70				
21	1.0	76	1.0			75	27	8	71				
22	.9	77	1.5			76	28	30	72				
23	1.6	78	1.0			77	30	31	73				
24	1.0	79	1.9			78	31	32	74				
25	5.0	80	.9			79	32	33	75				
26	1.7	81	1.0			80	33	36	76				
27	1.1	82	1.3			81	35	37	77				
28	2.1	83	1.0			82	36	38	78				
29	1.1	84	3.2			83	37	39	79				
30	4.8	85	.8			84	38	40	80				
31	1.0	86	1.0			85	39	41	81				
32	1.2	87	2.8			86	40	43	82				
33	1.6	88	1.6			87	41	44	83				
34	1.7	89	.9			89	42	45	84		2d		
35	5.6	90	1.3			90	43	46	85		Vi.		
36	.9	91	2.2			92	44	47	86				
37	1.3	92	7.0			94	45	48	87				
38	3.8	93	1.8			95	46	49	88				
39	9.0	94	1.1			96	47	51	89				
40	.9	95	1.0			97	48	52	90				
41	.7	96	5.5			98	49	53	91				
42	2.6	97	1.2			99	50	54	92				
43	1.2	98	1.8			100	51	56	95				
44	4.8	99	3.6			90	52	57	96				
45	1.0	100	1.1				53	58	97				
46	1.0	1Q	1.0				54	59	98				
47	1.2	2Q	1.3				56	60	99				
48	.8	3Q	2.0				57	61	100				
49	1.1						58	62	85				
50	.8						59	63					
51	.7						60	64					
52	.7						61	65					
53	1.4						62	66					
54	1.1						63	67					
55	1.3						1	68					

Observer - C.

SUMMARY.

Sound & syn. change	Word, phrase & idea comp.	Identity	Contrast	Co-existence	Predicate	Judgment of quality	Subordination
67	7	2		1	6	59	20
	14	3		11	9		61
	26	4		34	13		92
	27	5		42	16		3
	36	8		46	21		
	48	12		57	29		
	60	15		74	32		
	62	18		78	45		
	63	19		91	50		
	64	22		9	55		
	70	24			72		
	76	28			87		
	80	31	Identity		94		
	82	33	81		13		
	86	37	83				
	15	38	84		--		
		40	85		14		
		41	88				
		43	89				
		44	90				
		47	93				
		49	96				
		51	97				
		52	98				
		53	99				
		54	100				
		56					
		58	49				
		65					
		66					
		68					
		69					
		71					
		73					
		77					
		79					

Coordination	Supraordination	Egocentric	Ego. predicate	Subject relation	Object relation	Causality	Failure
	17			95			10
						23	25
						30	35
						75	39
						3	4

Observor - D. SUMMARY.

Consecutive or simultaneous ideas: Wd.	Time	Wd.	Time	Type of situation recalled: Particular: Visual	Particular: Other	General: Visual	General: Other	Accompanying imagery: Ar.	Vi.	Ki.	Cl.	2d	Nn
1	3.1	56	5.0	38	22	1	2	2	1	81	Cu.	Ar.	5
2	3.4	57	1.0	71	99	3	5	6	3		Cu.	37	33
3	6.4	58	1.2	96	2	4	6	7	11		Au.	50	53
4	1.0	59	1.7	3		11	7	8	16			69	65
5	4.0	60	.8			16	8	9	21			3	67
6	1.1	61	1.7			21	9	10	25				68
7	1.0	62	1.6			25	10	12	29				76
8	1.2	63	1.0			29	12	13	30				87
9	2.1	64	1.0			30	13	14	31				8
10	1.5	65	1.0			31	14	15	32				
11	2.7	66	3.1			32	15	17	36				
12	1.1	67	4.5			41	17	18	38				
13	1.3	68	1.0			45	18	19	41				
14	1.3	69	.8			46	19	20	45				
15	4.0	70	1.5			50	20	21	46				
16	1.1	71	2.0			51	23	22	50		1		
17	7.0	72	2.8			55	24	23	51				
18	5.0	73	.9			57	26	24	55				
19	4.4	74	1.1			58	27	26	57				
20	4.8	75	.8			60	28	27	58				
21	1.0	76	1.8			66	33	28	60				
22	1.2	77	4.9			70	34	29	66				
23	1.4	78	.9			74	35	32	70				
24	1.4	79	2.8			75	36	34	71				
25	1.6	80	.8			77	37	35	74				
26	1.0	81	.7			88	39	36	75				
27	1.0	82	4.8			9;	40	39	77				
28	3.8	83	1.8			93	42	40	88				
29	.9	84	2.0			95	43	42	91				
30	8.2	85	2.6			97	44	43	93				
31	1.9	86	1.7			30	47	44	95				
32	2.7	87	4.0				48	47	96				
33	.6	88	1.1				49	48	97				
34	1.2	89	1.0				52	49	33			2d	
35	1.2	90	1.4				53	51				Vi.	
36	1.0	91	1.0			Other	54	52					
37	3.3	92	1.4			83	56	54					
38	2.0	93	2.0			84	59	55	Ar.				
39	1.0	94	2.4			85	61	56	83				
40	1.4	95	1.0			86	62	57	84				
41	.8	96	1.4			87	63	58	85				
42	5.3	97	2.4			89	64	59	86				
43	6.2	98	3.0			90	65	61	89				
44	1.0	99	3.7			92	67	62	90				
45	2.8	100	1.0			94	68	63	91				
46	6.4	1Q	1.0			98	69	64	92				
47	1.1	2Q	1.45			100	72	72	94				
48	5.5	3Q	2.8			65	73	73	95				
49	1.0						76	74	96				
50	1.1						78	75	98				
51	1.8						79	77	99				
52	1.3						80	78	100				
53	9.0						81	79	69				
54	1.2						82	80					
55	1.6							82					

Observor - D.

SUMMARY.

Sound & syn. change	Word, phrase & idea comp.	Identity	Contrast	CO-existence	Predicate	Judgment of quality	Subordination
2	9	5	4	61	11	82	12
7	21	10	14	66	22		46
8	27	15	69	77	32		91
18	31	33	81	84	37		3
19	35	41	4	99	62		
23	45	48		5	94		
24	50	51			98		
25	80	59			7		
29	96	65			--		
34	9	67			8		
38		68					
39		70					
40		71					
43		76					
44		87					
47		92					
49		93					
52		97					
54		100					
55		19					
56							
57							
58							
63							
64							
72							
73							
74							
75							
78							
83							
85							
86							
89							
36 90							
95							

Coordination	Supraordination	Egocentric	Ego.predicate	Subject relation	Object relation	Causality	Failure
6	36				88		1
16	79						3
60							13
3	2						17
							20
							26
							28
							30
							42
							53
							10

SUMMARY.

Observor - E.

Consecutive or simultaneous ideas: Wd.	Time	Wd.	Time	Type of situation recalled: Particular: Visual	Particular: Other	General: Visual	General: Other	Accompanying Imagery: Ar.	Vi.	Ki.	Cl.	2d	Nn
1	1.7	56	1.7	3	4	1	2	1	1	9	Gu.	Ar.	
2	2.0	57	1.3	5	34	6	14	2	3	13	Gu.	10	
3	1.2	58	1.4	7	61	18	16	3	5	16	Au.	19	
4	1.1	59	1.3	8	70	21	35	4	4	42	6	22	
5	1.8	60	1.4	9	74	24	38	11	6	52	Gu;	48	
6	1.8	61	1.5	10	82	26	39	12	7	5	16	54	
7	2.2	62	1.4	11	84	29	40	14	8		Gu;	58	
8	2.4	63	1.8	12	90	33	46	18	9	Vi	29	62	
9	1.6	64	1.4	13	100	42	47	23	12	23	Gu;	63	
10	1.8	65	1.6	15	9	45	52	27	11	24	45	8	
11	1.4	66	2.4	17		50	53	28	14	26	Cu;		
12	2.2	67	1.1	19		57	55	31	18	27	50		
13	1.0	68	2.0	20		66	56	33	22	28	Cu;		
14	1.3	69	1.4	22		68	65	34	27	29	62		
15	1.9	70	2.0	23		69	67	35	28	30	Au;		
16	1.0	71	2.7	25		75	73	36	~~31~~	31	80		
17	1.7	72	1.8	27		79	76	38	~~33~~	32	Au;		
18	2.0	73	.9	28		80	77	39	~~34~~	33	7		
19	1.4	74	2.3	30		81	78	40	~~35~~	36			
20	1.3	75	2.3	31		91	83	46	~~36~~	37			
21	1.0	76	2.2	32		93	85	47	~~38~~	41			
22	1.4	77	2.0	36		94	86	53	~~39~~	42			
23	1.7	78	2.0	37		98	87	55	~~40~~	43			
24	1.7	79	1.9	41		99	89	56	~~46~~	44			
25	2.8	80	1.3	43		24	92	61	~~47~~	45			
26	1.3	81	2.7	44			95	65	~~53~~	49			
27	1.0	82	2.4	48			96	67	~~55~~	50			
28	3.0	83	1.1	49				69	~~56~~	51			
29	2.1	84	3.7	51			27	70	~~61~~	57			
30	1.4	85	2.9	54				71	~~65~~	58			
31	1.4	86	1.5	58				73	~~67~~	60			
32	3.0	87	2.5	59				74	~~69~~	62			
33	1.2	88	1.5	60				76	~~70~~	63			
34	4.0	89	1.8	62				77	~~71~~	66		2d	
35	1.3	90	2.2	63				78	~~73~~	68		Vi.	
36	.9	91	1.3	64				81	~~74~~	69		10	
37	2.9	92	1.6	71				82	~~76~~	71		17	
38	1.3	93	2.0	72				83	~~77~~	72		22	
39	1.2	94	1.9	88				84	~~78~~	75		25	
40	2.4	95	2.1	97				85	~~81~~	79		48	
41	2.8	96	2.2	40				86	~~82~~	80		54	
42	2.0	97	2.7					87	~~83~~	81		59	
43	1.4	98	3.7					89	~~84~~	88		62	
44	2.1	99	1.3					92	~~85~~	91		6	
45	1.0	100	2.7					94	~~86~~	93			
46	1.3	1Q	1.3					96	~~87~~	94			
47	1.6	2Q	1.7					100	~~89~~	97			
48	1.3	3Q	2.2					48	~~92~~	98			
49	1.7								~~94~~	99			
50	1.4								~~96~~	57			
51	1.4								13				
52	1.0								15				
53	1.4								18				
54	1.3								20				
55	1.3								19				
									21				

Observor - E.

SUMMARY.

Sound & syn. change	Word, phrase & idea comp.	Identity	Contrast	Co-existence	Predicate	Judgment of quality	Subordination
18	14	1	44	12	4	10	20
28	27	5	86	17	6		58
33	35	7		26	9		74
40	36	30		32	19		84
47	55	31		42	21		
56	70	53		43	22		
65	71	59		51	24		
69	81	73		64	29		
76		87		66	37		
78		90		68	45		
85		92		72	48		
96				79	50		
				88	54		
				91	57		
				94	60		
				97	61		
				99	62		
					75		
					77		
					89		
					95		
					98		
					100		
12	8	11	2	17	23		4

					24		

Coordination	Supraordination	Egocentric	Ego predicate	Subject relation	Object relation	Causality	Failure
3	15			8	13	67	2
11	39			38	16	93	52
25	41			83	23		
34	46				63		
49	80				82		
5	5			3	5	2	2

Observor - F. SUMMARY.

Consecutive or simultaneous ideas				Type of situation recalled: Particular		General		Accompanying Imagery					
Wd.	Time			Visual	Other	Visual	Other	Ar.	Vi.	Ki.	Cl.	2d	Nn
1	1.4	56	1.4	3	15	1		2	2	1: 42	Gu.	Ar.	
2	7.0	57	1.0	5	18	4		8	5	3	Cu.	17	
3	1.9	58	1.4	7	53	6		14	8	5	Au.	19	
4	1.1	59	1.6	22	69	9		17	11	7	47	23	
5	1.4	60	1.3	64		10		25	14	9	Au	30	
6	1.6	61	1.8		4	11		27	15	10	50	32	
7	1.3	62	1.2	5		12		28	18	11	Cu	39	
8	1.5	63	1.3			13		30	21	12	86	51	
9	1.7	64	1.4			16		33	22	13	Au	52	
10	3.0	65	1.0			19		34	25	16	100	69	
11	1.2	66	2.1			20		35	26	17	Au		
12	2.2	67	2.0			21		36	27	19	4	9	
13	2.7	68	1.2			23		37	28	20			
14	2.2	69	1.4			24		39	30	21			
15	3.2	70	1.0			26		40	31	22			
16	2.6	71	2.7			29		41	33	23		L	
17	1.2	72	1.5			31		46	34	24			
18	6.0	73	1.3			32		48	35	26			
19	1.2	74	1.5			38		49	36	29			
20	1.4	75	1.3			42		51	37	31			
21	1.0	76	1.2			43		52	40	32			
22	5.6	77	1.6			44		54	41	38			
23	2.9	78	1.6			45		55	46	42			
24	1.6	79	1.8			47		56	48	43			
25	1.6	80	1.0			50		57	49	44			
26	1.9	81	.8			63		58	54	45			
27	1.3	82	2.2			67		59	55	47			
28	1.5	83	1.6			72		60	56	50			
29	1.2	84	1.7			75		61	57	53			
30	3.6	85	1.2			78		62	58	63			
31	1.8	86	1.7			80		65	59	64			
32	1.3	87	1.3			98		66	60	67			
33	1.4	88	1.1			100		68	61	72			
34	3.0	89	1.0					70	62	75		2d	
35	1.2	90	1.8			33		71	64	78		Vi.	
36	1.0	91	1.1					73	65	80			
37	1.0	92	1.5					74	66	98			
38	1.8	93	3.8					76	68	100			
39	1.7	94	1.3					77	70				
40	1.3	95	1.1					79	71	38			
41	1.0	96	2.0					81	72				
42	1.2	97	1.2					82	73	Ar.			
43	1.4	98	1.3			Other		83	74	90			
44	2.9	99	1.2			96		84	76	91			
45	1.0	100	1.0			97		85	77	92			
46	.8	1Q	1.2			99		86	79	93			
47	.9	2Q	1.4					87	81	94			
48	5.5	3Q	1.8			58		88	82	95			
49	1.0							89	83	96			
50	1.3							90	84	97			
51	1.0							91	85	98			
52	1.4							92	86	99			
53	1.4							93	87	100			
54	1.1							94	88	66			
55	2.0							95	89				

Observor - F.

SUMMARY.

Sound & syn. change	Word, phrase & idea comp.	Identity	Contrast	CO-existence	Predicate	Judgment of quality	Subordination
28	6	1	4,	10	3		12
52	8	5	67	16	9		
	11	38	69	18	17		
	14	41	70	20	19		
	15	43	73	39	20		
	24	44	79	42	29		
	25	47	80	56	30		
	26	48	81	63	32		
	27	49	84	71	50		
	31	50	87	78	61		
	33	53	91	99			
	35	54					
	36	58					
	37	59					
	40	62					
	45	65					
	46	68					
	55	72					
	57	76					
	60	83					
	66	85					
	74	88					
	82	92					
	86	94					
	90	96					
	97						
	98						
	100						
2	28	25	11	11	10		

Coordination	Supraordination	Egocentric	Ego.predicate	Subject relation	Object relation	Causality	Failure
34	7			75	13	22	2
64				95		23	
89						77	
						93	
3				2		4	

Observor - G. SUMMARY.

Wd	Time		1	Particular: Visual	Particular: Other	General: Visual	General: Other	Au	Vi	Ki	Cl	2d	Nn
1	2.0	5	.0	1	5	2	10	5	1	35	Gu.	Ar	25
2	1.2	57	.7	3	7	9	21	6	2	44	Ou.	38	33
3	1.4	58	.8	4	41	12	25	10	3		Au	41	58
4	2.0	60	.6	6	59	14	31	11	4	2	45	49	64
5	1.3	61	0	8		16	33	13	6		Au	70	65
6	1..5	62	1 1	11	4	18	35	15	7		50	79	83
7	1.8	63	0	13		19	44	21	8		Cu	87	99
8	2.4	64	6	15		23	48	27	9			89	
9	1.5	65	9	17		29	49	31	11		2		7
10	1.2	66	8	20		32	52	35	12			7	
11	1.3	67	1 2	22		34	54	46	13				
12	1.0	68	1 7	24		36	56	48	14				
13	1.0	69	1 4	26		38	58	52	15				
14	2.4	70	1 1	27		39	64	53	16				
15	1.0	71	2.0	28		40	65	54	17				
16	1.4	72	1.6	30		42	67	56	18				
17	1.9	73	1.7	37		45	71	59	19		L		
18	1.4	74	1.5	43		46	79	67	20				
19	.9	75	.8	51		47	81	71	22				
20	1.2	76	1.3	68		50	82	80	23				
21	.9	77	1.4	72		51	83	81	24				
22	1.3	78	1 4	76		55	87	82	26				
23	1.6	79	2.0	78		57	89	85	27				
24	1.2	80	.8	84		60	92	91	28				
25	1.7	81	1.9	90		61	98	92	29				
26	2.0	82	1.4	97		62	99	98	30				
27	1.0	83	1.4			63			32				
28	.9	84	1.8	26		66	26	26	34	Vi			
29	1.0	85	1.7			69			36	77			
30	1.3	86	1.3			70			37	78			
31	1.0	87	1.5			73			38	80			
32	.8	88	.9			74			39	84			
33	1.2	89	1.6			75			40	85			
34	1.0	90	1.2			77			42	86	2d		
35	2.9	91	1.1			80			43	88	Vi.		
36	.6	92	.7			85			45	90			
37	1.0	93	.8			86			46	91			
38	1.0	94	1.1			88			47	93			
39	1.2	95	.6			91			50	94			
40	1.0	96	1.0			93			51	95			
41	.8	97	1.2			94			53	96			
42	1.1	98	2.1			95			55	97			
43	.8	99	.6			96			57	100			
44	1.0	100	1.4			100			60				
45	.7								61	71			
46	.8	1Q	.9			44			62				
47	.7	2Q	1.2						63				
48	1.0	3Q	1.5						66				
49	1.1								68				
50	2.0								69				
51	.7								70				
52	1.6								72				
53	1.3								73				
54	.8								74				
55	.7								75				
56	.9								76				

Observor - G.

SUMMARY.

Sound & syn. change	Word, phrase & idea comp.	Identity	Contrast	Co-existence	Predicate	Judgment of quality	Subordination
34	6	14	84	4	3		1
82	27	33		8	5		2
98	36	35		9	10		7
	37	38		11	16		12
	46	43		15	19		17
	68	47		20	28		18
	80	51		24	29		22
	89	54		25	30		39
		56		26	32		71
		57		41	40		72
		58		42	48		73
		62		44	49		74
		63		53	50		81
		65		59	55		91
		66		60	61		
		69		64	70		
		85		75	87		
		90		78	84		
		92		79			
		93		83			
		96		86			
		100		97			
				99			
3	8	22		23	18		14

Coordination	Supraordination	Egocentric	Ego. predicate	Subject relation	Object relation	Causality	Failure
				67	31	13	52
				95	76	21	
					88	23	
						45	
						77	
				2	3	5	

Observor - H.

SUMMARY.

Consecutive or simultaneous ideas				Type of situation recalled				Accompanying Imagery					
				Particular		General							
Wd.	Time			Visual	Other	Visual	Other	Au.	Vi.	Ki.	Cl.	2d.	Nn
1	1.7	56	.9	70	87	1	3	3	1	3	Gu.	Ar.	30
2	1.8	57	1.7	86		2	8	6	2	4	Cu.	32	
3	2.2	58	1.6	90		4	10	8	4	7	Au.	57	
4	1.6	59	1.4			5	11	10	5	8	40	77	
5	2.0	60	1.0	3		6	14	11	6	9	Cu	86	
6	2.3	61	1.0			7	15	17	7	13	56	93	
7	1.5	62	1.4			9	17	20	9	14	Au	98	
8	2.6	63	2.3			12	19	22	12	15		100	
9	1.6	64	1.6			13	20	24	13	16	2		
10	1.3	65	1.0			16	22	25	16	18		7	
11	1.0	66	1.1			18	25	27	18	19			
12	1.2	67	1.0			21	28	33	21	21			
13	1.1	68	1.3			23	30	34	23	22			
14	1.4	69	1.4			24	31	35	17	23			
15	1.4	70	1.7			26	33	36	26	28			
16	1.2	71	1.1			27	35	38	27	29	I.		
17	1.4	72	1.0			29	37	41	29	31			
18	1.2	73	1.2			32	38	47	32	32			
19	1.2	74	1.1			34	41	48	34	33			
20	1.3	75	1.3			36	43	51	36	34			
21	.9	76	1.6			39	44	55	39	36			
22	1.7	77	1.5			40	47	58	40	37			
23	2.0	78	1.0			42	48	62	42	42			
24	1.7	79	.9			45	51	63	49	43			
25	1.0	80	1.0			46	54	70	50	44			
26	1.4	81	1.0			49	56	81	52	45			
27	1.2	82	1.7			50	58	83	53	46			
28	1.4	83	1.4			52	59	85	55	49			
29	1.7	84	1.4			53	61	89	60	50			
30	4.0	85	1.1			55	62	92	66	51			
31	1.4	86	.8			57	63	94	69	52			
32	1.2	87	.9			60	64	97	70	54			
33	1.3	88	1.3			69	65		72	58			
34	1.2	89	.9			72	66	33	74	59		2d	
35	1.2	90	1.2			74	67		75	61	Ki	Vi.	
36	.9	91	1.0			75	68		80	63	87		
37	6.6	92	5.4			80	71		86	64	88		
38	.7	93	.8			95	73		88	65	93		
39	1.8	94	.7			99	76		90	66	94		
40	1.0	95	.8			39	77		95	67	95		
41	1.7	96	1.8				78		99	68	96		
42	1.3	97	.7			Other	79			69	98		
43	1.1	98	.8			98	81		41	71	99		
44	1.2	99	1.5			100	82			72	100		
45	1.7	100	.7			57	83			73			
46	1.4	1Q	1.0				84			74	63		
47	.9	2Q	1.3				85			75			
48	3.9	3Q	1.6				88			76			
49	1.4						89			77			
50	2.2						91			78			
51	1.7						92			79			
52	.9						93			81			
53	1.4						94			82			
54	1.4						96			84			
55	.9						97						

Observor - H. SUMMARY.

Sound & syn. change	Word, phrase & idea comp.	Identity	Contrast	Co-existence	Predicate	Judgment of quality	Subordination
34	6	14	4	2	5	96	1
85	11	15	7	10	19		12
92	24	28	79	17	50		22
	27	29	84	20	52		60
3	35	32	88	26	53		86
	36	33		42	54		
	38	40	5	46	57		5
	55	41		77	58		
	81	43		78	59		
		45		83	62		
	9	47		90	74		
		48		91	87		
		49		12	89		
		50			93		
		56			94		
		61			98		
		65			100		
		66					
		67			17		
		68			--		
		69			18		
		70					
		71					
		72					
		73					
		82					
		95					
		97					
		28					

Coordination	Supraordination	Egocentric	Ego. predicate	Subject relation	Object relation	Causality	Failure
25	39	3		13	18	9	30
64		8		16	63	21	31
80		44		75	76	23	37
3		3		3	3	99	3
						4	

Observor - I. SUMMARY.

Consecutive or simultaneous ideas: Wd.	Time	Wd.	Time	Type of situation recalled: Particular: Visual	Particular: Other	General: Visual	General: Other	Accompanying Imagery: Ar.	Vi.	Ki.	Cl.	2d	Nn
1	1.5	56	1.3	1	6	9	2	2	1		Gu.	Ar.	40
2	1.0	57	1.1	5	23	13	3	3	5		Gu.	22	
3	1.7	58	1.0	7	30	16	4	4	7		Au.	61	
4	.8	59	1.4	12	33	26	8	6	9		80	69	
5	1.6	60	1.5	14	35	36	10	8	12		Au		
6	5.0	61	1.0	20	39	38	11	10	13			3	
7	1.2	62	3.0	21	47	42	15	11	14				
8	1.4	63	1.8	24	60	51	17	15	16				
9	1.0	64	.8	25	66	80	18	17	20				
10	1.5	65	1.0	31	69	85	19	18	21				
11	1.2	66	1.9	32	76	88	22	19	24				
12	3.3	67	.9	34	82	91	27	23	25				
13	1.0	68	1.4	37	93	98	28	27	26				
14	1.2	69	2.5	41	94		29	28	31				
15	1.0	70	1.0	43	99	13	40	29	32				
16	1.9	71	1.1	45	100		44	30	34		I		
17	1.7	72	1.3	46			48	33	36				
18	2.8	73	1.9	50	16		49	35	37				
19	1.5	74	1.2	55			52	37	38				
20	1.2	75	3.2	63			53	39	42				
21	1.1	76	1.7	68			54	44	43				
22	1.1	77	1.5	70			56	47	46				
23	1.4	78	1.3	72			57	48	48				
24	1.6	79	1.7	74			58	49	50				
25	3.0	80	1.3	75			59	50	51				
26	1.3	81	1.3	77			61	52	54				
27	1.4	82	2.4	78			62	53	55				
28	3.0	83	1.9	81			64	54	63				
29	2.0	84	1.8	84			65	55	68				
30	1.3	85	1.5	86			67	57	69				
31	2.0	86	1.6	89			71	58	70				
32	2.0	87	1.7	90			73	59	72				
33	1.4	88	1.1	92			79	60	74				
34	5.7	89	1.1				83	61	75			2d	
35	1.1	90	1.3	33			87	62	77			Vi.	
36	1.3	91	1.4				95	64	78			69.	
37	1.0	92	1.0				96	65	80				
38	1.7	93	1.7				97	66	81				
39	1.5	94	1.0					67	84				
40	4.0	95	1.2				38	71	85				
41	1.6	96	1.7					72	86				
42	1.8	97	1.7					74	88				
43	1.4	98	1.7					76	89				
44	2.0	99	1.4					79	90				
45	1.6	100	1.2					83	91				
46	1.7							87	92				
47	3.3	1Q	1.13					89	93				
48	1.0	2Q	1.4					92	98				
49	1.4	3Q	1.8					93	48				
50	1.1							94					
51	2.2							95	Ar				
52	.8							96	100				
53	1.0							97	56				
54	2.8							98					
55	5.0							99					

Observor - I. SUMMARY.

Sound & syn. change	Word, phrase & idea comp.	Identity	Contrast	CO-existence	Predicate	Judgment of quality	Subordination
33	27	5	3	8	32	65	2
36	41	11	4	22	45	68	83
38	59	14	10	31	91		92
77	74	18	13	34		2	
98	86	23	15	44	3		3
96	94	24	17	49	--		
		25	19	54	5		
6	6	29	20	61			
		42	30	73			
		43	35	78			
		47	37	87			
		48	67	97			
		51	69				
		52		12			
		53	13				
		56					
		57					
		58					
		62					
		66					
		70					
		71					
		72					
		75					
		79					
		81					
		82					
		84					
		85					
		88					
		89					
		95					
		99					
		33					

Coordination	Supraordination	Egocentric	Ego.predicate	Subject relation	Object relation	Causality	Failure
9	1				26	76	6
15	7				63	93	28
21	12				90		40
39	46					2	55
50	80				3		
60							4
64	5						
100							
8							

Observor - J. SUMMARY.

Consecutive or simultaneous ideas				Type of situation recalled: Particular		General		Accompanying Imagery					
Wd.	Time			Visual	Other	Visual	Other	Au.	Vi.	Ki.	Cl.	2d	Nn
1	1.2	56	2.4	21	49	1	2	2	1	9	Gu	Ar	41
2	9.6	57	.8	25		6	3	3	6	33	Cu	5	47
3	.7	58	.9	33		7	4	8	7	42	Au	8	
4	.7	59	.9	37		11	5	10	11	81	4	9	2
5	.8	60	1.3	46		12	8	17	12	88	Au	15	
6	1.7	61	2.0			13	9	20	13		6	17	
7	1.8	62	2.0	5		14	10	24	14	5	Gu	19	
8	1.4	63	1.3			16	15	35	16		26	34	
9	.6	64	4.1			18	17	36	18		Au	39	
10	1.3	65	1.8			19	35	44	19		49	40	
11	1.1	66	1.8			20	41	48	20		Cu	53	
12	1.5	67	1.3			22	44	56	22		70	62	
13	1.2	68	1.0			23	47	58	23		Cu	69	
14	1.4	69	1.3			24	48	60	24		75	92	
15	.6	70	1.0			26	53	61	25		Or		
16	.7	71	1.1			27	56	64	26			113	
17	4.7	72	1.7			28	58	67	27		6		
18	1.3	73	1.0			29	59	73	28				
19	1.9	74	1.4			30	61	76	30				
20	1.2	75	1.1			31	62	78	31				
21	1.2	76	2.1			32	64	79	32				
22	1.5	77	1.9			34	67	83	33				
23	1.7	78	1.4			36	69	84	34				
24	1.2	79	2.0			38	73	86	36				
25	1.0	80	.8			39	76	90	37				
26	1.2	81	2.1			40	78	94	38				
27	1.9	82	1.2			42	79	99	39				
28	1.0	83	1.9			43	81	100	40				
29	.8	84	1.5			45	83		42				
30	1.9	85	1.9			51	84	28	43				
31	1.2	86	1.0			50	86		45				
32	1.3	87	.9			52	90		46				
33	1.3	88	1.4			54	92		49				
34	1.4	89	1.7			55	94		50			2d	
35	.9	90	2.0			57	99		51			Vi.	
36	.8	91	.9			60	100		52			21	
37	.9	92	3.5			63			54				
38	.7	93	1.1			65	36		55				
39	1.3	94	1.8			66			57				
40	1.3	95	1.0			68			60				
41	1.0	96	2.0			70	Visual		63	Vi			
42	1.8	97	.9			71	96		65	89			
43	1.0	98	1.4			72	97		66	91			
44	1.6	99	2.5			74	98		68	93			
45	.7	100	1.0			75			70	95			
46	1.2					77	58		71	96			
47	1.1	1Q	1.0			80			74	97			
48	1.1	2Q	1.25			82			75	98			
49	.7	3Q	1.7			85			77				
50	.7					87			80	62			
51	.8					88			82				
52	.7					89			85				
53	1.7					9;			87				
54	1.1					93			88				
55	1.7					95			29				

Observor-J.

SUMMARY.

Sound & syn. change	Word, phrase & idea comp.	Identity	Contrast	Co-existence	Predicate	Judgment of quality	Subordination
42	36	8	19	9	6	3	32
76	39	10	20	18	11	50	87
	48	12	30	46	34	63	
2	60	14	33	62	40		2
	67	17	35	85	59	3	
	86	22	37		65		
	94	24	38	5	71		
		26	53		74		
	7	31	64		97		
		41	69				
		44	77		9		
		47	79		--		
		49	84		12		
		51	91				
		52	99				
		54	100				
		55					
		56	16				
		57					
		58					
		66					
		68					
		70					
		73					
		82					
		93					
		89					
		90					
		92					
		95					
		98					
		31					

Coordination	Supraordination	Egocentric	Ego-predicate	Subject relation	Object relation	Causality	Failure
1	80			75	61	23	2
13					88	28	4
16						78	5
21					2	96	7
25							15
27						4	
29							5
43							
45							
72							
81							
93							
12							

Observor - K.'.

SUMMARY.

Consecutive or simultaneous ideas				Type of situation recalled				Accompanying Imagery					
				Particular		General							
Wd.	Time			Visual	Other	Visual	Other	Ar.	Vi.	Ki.	Ol.	2d	Nn
1	1.4	56	1.7	7	73	1	..35	.6	1	5	Gu.	Ar.	
2	1.2	57	.8	16		2	38	9	2	9	Ou.	16	
3	1.3	58	.8	30		3	47	10	3	29	Au.	17	
4	1.1	59	.8	44		4	59	14	4	42	.3	19	
5	3.2	60	1.9	83		5	61	31	5	4	Au	20	
6	.7	61	1.2	86		6	71	36	6	88	4	22	
7	2.7	62	.7			8	76	38	7	93	Au	23	
8	1.1	63	.9	7		9	79	46	8		17	30	
9	1.0	64	1.0			10	87	60	9	7	Au	32	
10	1.0	65	1.9			11	92	61	10		21	35	
11	1.0	66	1.6			12	93	65	11		Or	37	
12	1.0	67	1.0			13	94	73	12		29	43	
13	1.0	68	.7			14	96	74	13		01	47	
14	.8	69	1.2			15	98	79	14		29	50	
15	1.3	70	.9			17	99	96	15		Cu	52	
16	1.4	71	1.2			18	100	98	16		66	54	
17	1.1	72	1.0			19		100	17		Au	55	
18	1.2	73	1.0			20	15		18		80	57	
19	1.3	74	.7			2;		17	19		Au	v58	
20	.7	75	1.3			22			20			59	
21	.7	76	.7			23			21	Vi	8	62	
22	1.3	77	.9			24	Visual		22	60		63	
23	1.4	78	2.o			25	65		23	62		64	
24	1.7	79	1.2			26	66		24	63		67	
25	2.6	80	.7			27	67		25	64		68	
26	1.2	81	1.0			28	68		26	66		70	
27	2.6	82	.8			29	69		27	67		71	
28	1.4	83	1.1			31	70		28	68		72	
29	.8	84	1.3			32	72		29	69		76	
30	.9	85	1.9			33	74		30	70		77	
31	1.7	86	1.0			34	75		31	72	2d	78	
32	.9	87	.8			36	77		32	74	Ar	82	
33	.6	88	1.0			37	78		33	75	84	83	
34	1.2	89	1.0			39	80		34	77	85	2d	
35	1.3	90	1.0			40	81		36	78	87	Vi.	
36	.6	91	.6			41	82		37	80	89	44	
37	.8	92	1.3			42	84		39	81	90		
38	1.3	93	1.4			43	85		40	82	92		
39	2.4	94	1.1			46	88		41	83	93		
40	1.0	95	.6			45	89		42	84	94		
41	1.2	96	3.4			48	90		43	85	95		
42	.9	97	.7			49	91		44	86	97		
43	.6	98	1.0			50	95		45	88	99		
44	2.7	99	1.0			51	97		46	89			
45	.5	100	3.9			52			48	90	43		
46	2.8					53	77		49	91			
47	1.0	1Q	.83			54			50	95			
48	2.8	2Q	1.0			55			51	97			
49	1.4	3Q	1.3			56			52				
50	.8					57			53	82			
51	1.0					58			54				
52	.7					60			55				
53	1.2					62			56				
54	1.0					63			57				
55	1.2					64			58				

Observor - K.

SUMMARY.

Sound & syn. change	Word, phrase & idea comp.	Identity	Contrast	CO-existence	Predicate	Judgment of quality	Subordination
78	6	1	53	10	3	19	22
79	7	65		18	4	59	48
96	9	91		20	13	95	2
98	11	3		26	14	3	
4	36			31	15		
	45			35	28		
	50			42	29		
	55			46	32		
	64			60	37		
	74			61	43		
	86			71	52		
	94			83	54		
	12			12	57		
					58		
					66		
					68		
					69		
					70		
					73		
					81		
					82		
					87		
					89		
					90		
					92		
					93		
					97		
					27		
					--		
					30		

Coordination	Supraordination	Egocentric	Ego.predicate	Subject relation	Object relation	Causality	Failure
24	12			47	8	21	2
49	16			67	23	34	5
2	17			72	30	51	44
	25			76	33	3	75
	27			77	56		4
	38			84	62		
	39			94	63		
	41			99	85		
	80			8	88		
	100				9		
	10						

Observor - L. SUMMARY.

Wd.	Time	Wd.	Time	Particular Visual	Particular Other	General Visual	General Other	Ar.	Vi.	Ki.	Cl.	2d.	Fn
Consecutive or simultaneous ideas				Type of situation recalled				Accompanying Imagery					
1	1.7	56	3.0	11	26	1	2	.2	1	.9	Gu.	Ar.	
2	1.9	57	1.4	33	34	3	4	4	3	75	Cu.	19	
3	2.4	58	1.7	35	87	5	8	5	5		Au.	20	
4	1.2	59	1.7	37	96	6	14	6	6	2	29	22	
5	1.3	60	3.0	45		7	15	8	7		Cu	74	
6	1.9	61	2.1	46	4	9	20	10	9				
7	1.7	62	1.7	47		10	22	14	10			4	
8	1.6	63	1.8	50		12	23	15	11				
9	2.4	64	2.4	64		13	25	17	12				
10	2.0	65	1.7	67		16	32	18	13				
11	.9	66	1.6	71		17	38	23	16				
12	1.0	67	1.6	73		18	39	25	17				
13	.8	68	2.1	74		19	40	26	18				
14	.9	69	3.3	77		21	41	27	19				
15	2.5	70	2.6	81		24	44	28	21				
16	1.2	71	1.3	84		27	48	32	24			L	
17	1.7	72	1.2	94		28	49	34	27				
18	1.2	73	3.7	97		29	51	38	28				
19	4.2	74	1.7			30	54	39	29				
20	1.3	75	1.1	18		31	56	40	30				
21	1.3	76	2.3			36	58	41	31				
22	1.9	77	2.5			42	59	43	33				
23	1.7	78	1.3			43	65	44	35				
24	1.0	79	2.7			52	66	48	36				
25	1.7	80	1.3			53	70	49	37				
26	1.4	81	2.4			55	72	51	42				
27	1.6	82	1.2			57	76	54	43				
28	13.3	83	1.4			60	78	56	45				
29	1.5	84	1.5			61	79	58	46				
30	1.0	85	1.8			62	80	59	47				
31	1.1	86	1.4			63	82	60	50				
32	1.7	87	1.8			68	83	65	52				
33	2.7	88	1.2			69	85	66	53				
34	1.3	89	2.1			75	86	70	55			2d	
35	1.9	90	1.8			88	90	71	57			Vi.	
36	1.0	91	1.1			89	91	72	60				
37	1.9	92	2.2			95	92	76	61				
38	1.2	93	3.0			98	93	78	62				
39	1.5	94	2.3				99	79	63				
40	1.1	95	1.0			38	100	80	64				
41	1.6	96	2.0					82	67				
42	1.3	97	1.3				40	83	68	Vi.			
43	1.5	98	1.3					85	69	98			
44	1.9	99	2.0					86	71				
45	1.3	100	1.4					87	73	56			
46	2.0							90	74				
47	2.0	1Q	1.3					91	75				
48	1.6	2Q	1.7					92	77				
49	1.4	3Q	2.3					93	81				
50	1.3							96	84				
51	1.2							98	88				
52	1.0							99	89				
53	1.9							100	94				
54	1.3							53	95				
55	1.5								97				

Observor - L. SUMMARY.

Sound & syn. change	Word, phrase & idea comp.	Identity	Contrast	CO-existence	Predicate	Judgment of quality	Subordination
18	5	15	4	10	1	9	22
65	6	23	67	20	11	48	92
82	8	41	77	30	24	73	96
83	14	43	91	31	28	85	97
93	27	49		33	29	100	
98	32	51	4	46	39		4
99	37	52		59	40	5	
	38	53		63	55		
7	60	54		64	57		
	70	56		72	69		
	71	58		75	81		
	74	66		78			
	76	68			11		
	86	95		12			
	89				--		
	90	14			16		
	94						
	17						

Coordination	Supraordination	Egocentric	Ego. predicate	Subject relation	Object relation	Causality	Failure
16	12	3		13	2	7	19
17	42			35	62	21	
25	45			36	88	26	
44	50			47		34	
79	80			61	3	84	
87							
	5			5		5	
6							

Lightning Source UK Ltd.
Milton Keynes UK
UKHW012006221118
332793UK00010B/1877/P

9 780282 963828